SOLDIER E: SAS

SNIPER FIRE IN BELFAST

D0410641

SOLDIER E: SAS

SNIPER FIRE
IN BELFAST

Shaun Clarke

06018570

First published in Great Britain 1993
22 Books, 2 Sheldon Way, Larkfield, Maidstone, Kent

Copyright © 1993 by 22 Books

The moral right of the author has been asserted

A CIP catalogue record for this book is available from the
British Library

ISBN 1 898125 06 6

10 9 8 7 6 5 4 3 2 1

Typeset by Hewer Text Composition Services, Edinburgh
Printed in Great Britain by Cox and Wyman Limited, Reading

Prelude

Martin was hiding in a shallow scrape when they found him. He plunged into despair when he heard their triumphant shouting, then he was grabbed by the shoulders and jerked roughly up on to his knees.

The rain was lashing down over the wind-blown green fields, and he caught only a glimpse of the shadowy men in olive-green fatigues, carrying a variety of weapons and moving in to surround him, before he was blindfolded, bound by hands and feet, and thrown into the back of their truck like so much dead meat.

'Face down in the fucking mud,' one of them said, 'digging through to Australia.' The others laughed. 'Looks a bit on the damp side, doesn't he? That should save him embarrassment. We won't notice the stains when the bugger starts pissing his pants — and that won't take long, I'll bet.'

Lying on his side on the floor of the truck, feeling the occasional soft kick from the boots of the men sitting above him, Martin had to choke back his panic and keep control of himself.

After so long, he thought. *After so much. Don't lose it all now . . .*

The door on the driver's side of the truck slammed shut, then the engine coughed into life and the vehicle rattled across the hilly terrain, bumped over what Martin judged to be the rough edge of the field, then moved straight ahead along a proper road. Still in despair, though knowing he hadn't lost all yet, he took deep, even breaths, forcing his racing heart to settle down.

When someone's body rolled into his and he heard a nervous coughing, he realized with a shameful feeling of relief that he wasn't the only one they had caught.

'Shit!' he whispered.

'What was that, boyo?' one of his captors asked in a mocking manner. 'Did I hear filthy language from down there?'

'Take off this bloody blindfold,' Martin said. 'You don't really need that.'

'Feeling a bit uncomfortable, are you? A bit disorientated? Well, you better get used to it, you stupid prat, because that blindfold stays on. Now shut your mouth and don't speak until you're spoken to.'

The other tethered man rolled away from Martin, coughing uncomfortably. 'We don't have to . . .' he began.

2

'Put a sock in it,' the same captor said, leaning down to roll the man over and somehow silence him. Even as Martin was wondering what the man was doing, a cloth was wrapped tightly around his mouth and tied in a knot at the back of his head. 'Now you're dumb as well as blind,' the man said. 'That should teach you not to open your trap when it's not called for.'

'Have you pissed your pants yet?' another voice asked. 'It's hard to tell, you're both so wet all over. Hope you're not feeling cold, lads.'

Some of the men laughed. 'Fucking SAS,' another man said contemptuously. 'Supposed to be impossible to find and these pricks lie there waiting to be picked up. If this is the best they can manage, they must be fit for the Girl Guides.'

The last remark raised a few more laughs and made Martin feel even worse, adding humiliation to his despair and increasing his fear of what might be to come.

You haven't lost it all yet, he told himself. *Just try to stay calm, in control. Don't let them get to you. Don't let fear defeat you.*

It was easier to contemplate than it was to put into practice. Indeed, as the truck growled and shook beneath him, its hard boards seeming to hammer him, he became increasingly aware of his blindfold and gag, which in turn made him feel claustrophobic and unbearably helpless. As the blindfold was also covering his ears, he was practically deaf, dumb and blind. That forced him deeper into himself and made him strain to break out. This feeling was not eased by the cruel mockery of his captors as the truck growled and rattled along the road.

'A big, brave British soldier?' one of his captors said, prodding him in the ribs with his boot. 'Found hiding face down in the mud. Not so big and brave now, boys.'

'Might be big in unseen places. Might be brave with what's hidden.'

'That'll be the day. A pair of English nancy boys. A pair of uniformed British poofters tryin' to keep real men down. Well, when we get where we're goin', we'll find out what they're made of. I'm lookin' forward to that.'

It's not real, Martin thought, trying to stop himself from shivering, his soaked clothing starting to freeze and his exhaustion now compounded by despair at being caught. *Bear in mind that nothing is real, that nothing can break you. Just don't make a mistake.*

After what seemed like an eternity, the truck came to a halt, the back was dropped down, and Martin was roughly hauled to his feet and dragged down to the ground, where they deliberately rolled him in the mud a few times, then stood him up in the wind and rain. Someone punched him lightly on the back of his neck, urging him forward. But as his ankles were still tethered together, allowing only minimal movement, they lost patience and two of them dragged him by the armpits across what seemed to be an open space – the wind was howling across it, lashing the rain into his face – then up steps, onto a porch. He heard doors squeaking open, felt warmer air reach his face, then was dragged in to where there was no wind or rain and the warmth was a blessing. His boots scraped over what seemed like linoleum, then they dragged him around a corner, along another straight stretch, then through another door – again he heard it squeaking as it opened – and at last pushed him down into a chair.

Stay calm, he thought desperately. *Don't make any mistakes. It all depends on what you say or don't say, so don't let them trick you. Don't panic. Don't break.*

'What a filthy specimen,' someone said contemptuously. 'He looks like he's been taking a swim in his own piss and shit.'

'Just mud and rain, sir,' another man said. 'Not the gentleman's fault, his appearance. The natural elements, is all.'

'Where did you find him?'

'Belly down in the mud. Trying to blend in with the earth in the hope that we'd miss him. Fat chance of that, sir.'

'The dumb British shit. He must think we're all halfwits. Do we talk to him now or let him dry out?'

'He won't smell so bad when he dries out.'

'That's true enough. Hood him.'

The cloth was removed from Martin's mouth, letting him breathe more easily. No sooner had he begun to do so than a hood was slipped over his head and tightened around his neck with a cord, making him feel even more claustrophobic. A spasm of terror whipped through him, then passed away again.

Breathe deeply and evenly, he thought. *You're not going to choke. They're just trying to panic you.*

'My name is Martin Renshaw,' he said, just to hear the sound of his own voice. 'My rank is . . .'

A hand pressed over his mouth and pushed his head back until the hard chair cut painfully into his neck.

'When we want your name, rank, serial number and date of birth we'll ask for it,' the colder voice said. 'Don't speak again unless spoken to. We'll now leave you to dry out. Understood?'

Martin nodded.

'That's a good start. Now be a good boy.'

Their footsteps marched away, the door opened and slammed shut, then there was only the silence and his own laboured breathing. Soon he thought he could hear his heart beating, ticking off every second, every terrible minute.

As the hours passed he dried out, and his clothing became sticky, though it could have been sweat. Not knowing if it was one or the other only made him feel worse. His exhaustion, already considerable before his capture, was now attacking his mind. His thoughts slipped like faulty gears, his fear alternated with defiance, and when he started drifting in and out of consciousness it was only the cramp in his tightly bound arms that kept him awake.

He was slipping gratefully into oblivion when someone kicked his chair over. The shock was appalling, jolting him awake, screaming, though he didn't hit the floor. Instead, someone laughed and grabbed the back of the chair to tip him upright again. The blood had rushed to his head and the panic had almost made him snap, but he took a deep breath and controlled himself, remembering that the hood was still over his head and that his feeling of suffocation was caused by that, as well as by shock.

'So sorry,' a man said, sounding terribly polite and English. 'A little mishap. Slip of the foot. I trust you weren't hurt.'

'No,' Martin said, shocked by the breathless sound of his own voice. 'Could you remove this hood? Its really . . . '

The chair went over again and stopped just before hitting the floor. This time they held him in that position for some time, letting the blood run to his head, then tipped him upright again and let his breathing settle.

'We ask the questions,' the polite gentleman said, 'and you do the answering. Now could you please tell us who else was with you in that field.'

Martin gave his name, rank, service number and date of birth.

The chair was kicked back, caught and tipped upright, then someone else bawled in Martin's face: 'We don't want to know that!'

After getting his breath back, Martin gave his name, rank, service number and date of birth, thinking, *This isn't real.*

It became real enough after that, with a wide variety of questions either politely asked or bawled, the polite voice alternating with the bullying one, and the chair being thrown back and jerked up again, but getting lower to the floor every time. Eventually, when Martin, despite his surging panic, managed to keep repeating only his name, rank, serial number and date of birth, they gave up on the chair and dragged him across the room to slam him face first into what seemed like a bare wall. There, the ropes around his ankles were released and he was told to spread his legs as wide as possible, almost doing the splits.

'Don't move a muscle,' he was told by the bully.

He stood like that for what seemed a long time, until his thighs began to ache intolerably and his whole body sagged.

'Don't move!' the bully screamed, slamming

Martin's face into the wall again and forcing him to straighten his aching spine. 'Stay as still as the turd you are!'

'We're sorry to be so insistent,' the polite one added, 'but you're not helping at all. Now, regarding what you were doing out there in the fields, do please tell us . . .'

It went on and on, with Martin either repeating his basic details or saying: 'I cannot answer that question.' They shouted, cajoled and bullied. They made him stand in one position until he collapsed, then let him rest only long enough to enable them to pick another form of torture that did not involve beating.

Martin knew what they were doing, but this wasn't too much help, since he didn't know how long it would last, let alone how long he might endure it. Being hooded only made it worse, sometimes making him feel that he was going to suffocate, at other times making him think that he was hallucinating, but always depriving him of his sense of time. It also plunged him into panics based solely on the fact that he no longer knew left from right and felt mentally and physically unbalanced.

Finally, they left him, letting him sleep on the floor, joking that they were turning out the light, since he couldn't see that anyway. He lay there for an eternity — but perhaps only minutes — now yearning just to sleep, too tired to sleep, and whispering his name, rank, serial number and date of birth over and over, determined not to make a mistake when repeating it or, worse, say more than that. The only words he kept in mind other than those were: 'I cannot answer that question.' He had dreams – they may have been hallucinations – and had no idea of how long he .had been lying there where they returned to torment him.

They asked Martin if he smoked and, when he said no, blew a cloud of smoke in his face. While he was coughing, they asked him more questions. When he managed, even through his delirium, to stick to his routine answers, one of them threw him back on the freezing floor and said: 'Let's feed the bastard to the dogs.'

They stripped off his clothing, being none too gentle, then left him to lie there, shivering with cold, almost sobbing, but controlling himself by endlessly repeating his name, rank, serial number and date of birth.

He almost lost control again when he heard dogs barking, snarling viciously, and hammering their paws relentlessly on the closed door.

Was it real dogs or a recording? Surely, they wouldn't . . . Who? By now he was too tired to think straight, forgetting why he was there, rapidly losing touch with reality, his mind expanding and contracting, his thoughts swirling in a pool of light and darkness in the hood's stifling heat.

A recording, was the thought he clung to. *Must not panic or break*.

The door opened and snarling dogs rushed in, accompanied by the shouting of men.

The men appeared to be ordering the dogs back out. When the dogs were gone, the door closed again.

Silence.

Then somebody screamed: 'Where are you based?'

It was like an electric bolt shooting through Martin's body, making him twitch and groan. He started to tell them, wanted to tell them, and instead said: 'I cannot answer that question.'

'You're a good boy,' the civilized English voice said. 'Too stubborn for your own good.'

This time, when they hoisted him back on to the chair, he was filled with a dread that made him forget everything except the need to keep his mouth shut and make no mistakes. No matter what they said, no matter what they did, he would not say a word.

'What's the name of your squadron commander?' the bully bawled.

'I cannot answer that question,' Martin said, then methodically gave his name, rank, serial number and date of birth.

The silence that followed seemed to stretch out for ever, filling Martin with a dread that blotted out most of his past. Eventually the English-sounding voice said: 'This is your last chance. Will you tell us more or not?'

Martin was halfway through reciting his routine when they whipped off the hood.

Light blinded him.

1

'I still don't think we should do it,' Captain Dubois said, even as he hung his neatly folded OGs in his steel locker and started putting on civilian clothing. 'It could land us in water so hot we'd come out like broiled chicken.'

'We're doing it,' Lieutenant Cranfield replied, tightening the laces on his scuffed, black-leather shoes and oblivious to the fact that Captain Dubois was his superior officer. 'I'm fed up being torn between Army Intelligence, MI6, the RUC and even the "green slime",' he said, this last being the Intelligence Corps. 'If we come up with anything, as sure as hell one lot will approve, the other will disapprove, they'll argue for months, and in the end not a damned thing will be done. Well, not this time. I'm going to take that bastard out by myself. As for MI5 . . .'

Cranfield trailed off, too angry for words. After an uneasy silence, Captain Dubois said tentatively, 'Just because Corporal Phillips committed suicide . . .'

'Exactly. So to hell with MI5.'

Corporal Phillips had been one of the best of 14 Intelligence Company's undercover agents, infiltrating the most dangerous republican ghettos of Belfast and collecting invaluable intelligence. A few weeks earlier he had handed over ten first-class sources of information to MI5 and within a week they had all been assassinated, one after the other, by the IRA.

Apart from the shocking loss of so many watchers, including Phillips, the assassinations had shown that MI5 had a leak in its system. That leak, as Cranfield easily discovered, was their own source, Shaun O'Halloran, who had always been viewed by 14 Intelligence Company as a hardline republican, therefore unreliable. Having ignored the advice of 14 Intelligence Company and used O'Halloran without its knowledge, MI5, instead of punishing him, had tried to save embarrassment by simply dropping him and trying to cover his tracks.

Cranfield, still shocked and outraged by the death of ten men, as well as the subsequent suicide of the conscience-stricken Phillips, was determined that their betrayer, O'Halloran, would not walk away scot-free.

'A mistake is one thing,' he said, placing his foot back on the floor and grabbing a grey civilian's jacket from his locker, 'but to believe that you can trust someone with O'Halloran's track record is pure bloody stupidity.'

'They weren't to know that he was an active IRA member,' Dubois said, studying himself in the mirror and seeing a drab civilian rather than the SAS officer he actually was. 'They thought he was just another tout out to make a few bob.'

'Right,' Cranfield said contemptuously. 'They *thought*. They should have bloody well checked.'

Though nervous about his famously short-fused SAS officer, Captain Dubois understood his frustration.

For the past year sharp divisions had been appearing between the two main non-military Intelligence agencies: MI6 (the secret intelligence service run by the Commonwealth and Foreign Office, never publicly acknowledged) and MI5, the Security Service openly charged with counter-espionage. The close-knit, almost tribal nature of the RUC, the Royal Ulster Constabulary, meant that its Special Branch was also running its own agents with little regard for Army needs or requirements. RUC Special Branch, meanwhile, was running its own, secret cross-border contacts with the Irish Republic's Gardai Special Branch. Because of this complex web of mutually suspicious and secretive organizations, the few SAS men in the province, occupying key intelligence positions at the military HQ in Lisburn and elsewhere, were often exposed to internecine rivalries when trying to co-ordinate operations against the terrorists.

Even more frustrating was the pecking order.

While SAS officers attempted to be the cement between mutually mistrustful allies, soldiers from other areas acted as Military Intelligence Officers (MIOs) or Field Intelligence NCOs (Fincos) in liaison with the RUC. Such men and women came from the Intelligence Corps, Royal Military Police, and many other sources. The link with each RUC police division was a Special Military Intelligence Unit containing MIOs, Fincos and Milos (Military Intelligence Liaison Officers). An MIO working as part of such a unit could find himself torn by conflicting responsibilities to the RUC, Army Intelligence and MI6.

That is what had happened to Phillips. Though formally a British Army 'Finco' answerable to Military Intelligence, he had been intimidated by members of the Security Service into routeing his information to his own superiors via MI5. In doing so he had innocently sealed his own fate, as well as the fate of his ten unfortunate informants.

No wonder Cranfield was livid.

Still, Dubois felt a little foolish. As an officer of the British Army serving with 14 Intelligence Company, he was Cranfield's superior by both rank and position, yet Lieutenant Cranfield, one of a small number of SAS officers attached to the unit, ignored these fine distinctions and more or less did what he wanted. A flamboyant character, even by SAS standards, he had been in Northern Ireland only two months, yet already had garnered himself a reputation as a 'big timer', someone working out on the edge and possessed of extreme braggadocio, albeit with brilliant flair and matchless courage. While admiring him, for the latter qualities, Dubois was nervous about Cranfield's cocksure attitude, which he felt would land him in trouble sooner or later.

'We'll be in and out in no time,' Cranfield told him, clipping a holstered 9mm Browning High Power handgun to his belt, positioned halfway around his waist, well hidden by the jacket. 'So stop worrying about it. Are you ready?'

'Yes,' Dubois said, checking that his own High Power was in the cross-draw position.

'Right,' Cranfield said, 'let's go.'

As they left the barracks, Dubois again felt a faint flush of humiliation, realizing just how much he liked and admired Cranfield and had let himself be won over by his flamboyance. Though a former Oxford boxing blue and Catholic Guards officer, Dubois was helplessly awed by the fact that his second-in-command, Lieutenant Randolph 'Randy' Cranfield, formerly of the King's Own Scottish Borderers and the Parachute Regiment, had gone to Ampleforth where the founder of the SAS, David Stirling, had also been educated, and was widely admired for his daring – some would say reckless – exploits.

Dubois had his own brand of courage, which he had often displayed in the mean streets of Belfast or the 'bandit country' of Armagh, but he was basically conservative in outlook and helplessly admiring of those less inhibited. He had therefore gradually become Cranfield's shadow, rather than his leader, and recognition of this fact made him uncomfortable.

They entered what looked like a normal army compound, surrounded by high walls of corrugated iron, with watch-towers and electronically controlled gates guarded on both sides with reinforced sangars. These stone walls were high because the IRA's flavour of the month was the Russian-made RPG 7 short-range anti-tank weapon, which could hurl a rocket-propelled grenade in an arc with an effective range of 500 metres. With walls so high, however, the IRA would have to come dangerously close to the base before they could gain the required elevation for such an attack. The walls kept them at bay.

'Another bleak day in Armagh,' Cranfield said. 'God, what I'd give for some sunshine and the taste of sangria!'

'In January in Northern Ireland,' Dubois replied, 'I can't even imagine that. But I know that I'd prefer the heat of Oman to this bloody place.'

'Some of the others arriving next week have just come from there,' Cranfield said, 'which means they'll be well blooded, experienced in desert survival, filled with the humane values of the hearts-and-minds campaign . . .' – he paused for dramatic effect — 'and completely out of sorts here.'

'Yes,' Dubois agreed glumly. 'We'll have to firm them up quickly. And being attached to us won't make them too happy either. They'll think they've been RTU'd back to the regular Army.'

'They should be so lucky!' Cranfield exclaimed, shaking his head and chuckling ruefully. 'We should *all* be so lucky! Instead, we're with 14 Intelligence Company, in the quicksand of too many conflicting groups. We're neither here nor there, Jeremy.'

'No, I suppose not.'

Though 14 Intelligence Company was a reconnaissance unit, it had been given the cover title, 4 Field Survey Troop, Royal Engineers, but was also known as the Northern Ireland Training and Tactics team. Located in the army compound Dubois and Cranfield were visiting, it was equipped with unmarked, civilian 'Q' cars and various non-standard weapons, including the Ingram silenced sub-machine-gun. The camp was shared with a British Army Sapper unit.

'Look,' Cranfield said impatiently as they crossed the parade ground, from the barracks to the motor pool, in the pearly-grey light of morning, 'what we're doing isn't that unusual. I mean, six months ago we crossed the border to pick up an IRA commander and deposit him back in Northern Ireland, to be arrested by the RUC and brought to trial. Though a lot of people cried out in protest, that murderous bastard eventually got thirty years. Was it worth it or not?'

'It was worth it,' Dubois admitted, studying the low grey sky over the green fields of Armagh and longing for a holiday in the sun, as Cranfield had suggested.

'Right,' Cranfield said as they entered the busy motor pool, which reeked of petrol and was, as usual, filled with the roaring of engines being tested. 'Since that damned power struggle between Five and Six, Major Fred has repeatedly crossed the border wearing dirty jeans, bearded, and carrying a false driving licence issued in Dublin. We're not alone in this, Jeremy.'

'Major Fred' was an MI0 attached to Portadown Police HQ. Almost as disdainful of MI5 and MI6 as was Cranfield, he was also as daring in defying both of those organizations and going his own way. As the value of what he was doing had yet to be ascertained, Cranfield's citing of him as an example of what was admirable in the muddy, dangerous waters of intelligence gathering in bandit country was in no way encouraging to Dubois.

'I'm not interested in Major Fred,' he said. 'Let him worry the Portadown lot. I'm only interested in 14 Intelligence Company and how it might be adversely affected by what you're planning to do.'

'There won't be any adverse effects. We've had those already. We can't do any worse than ten murdered and one suicide. At the very least we'll deny the IRA what they think is a propaganda victory. It's not purely personal.'

I'll bet, Dubois thought. 'I just wish the ceasefire hadn't ended,' he said, not wanting his silence to reveal that he was actually nervous.

'Why?' Cranfield replied. 'It was all nonsense anyway, inspired by the usual, idiotic rivalry between MI5 and MI6. I mean, what did it all amount to? During a raid on an IRA headquarters in Belfast, security forces discover a "doomsday" contingency plan for counter-attack on Protestant areas should there be a repetition of August '69. Dismayed, the Foreign Office, including MI6, seeks a political solution that involves secret contacts with the IRA. The IRA plays along. As they do so, MI5 insist that the terrorists are merely seeking a breathing space. Knowledge of the doomsday plan then gives MI5 a perfect chance to discredit political contacts. Bingo! The ceasefire collapses and we're back in business. Pull the plug on MI5 and we'd all live in a better world.'

They stopped by a red Morris Marina, one of the Q cars, equipped with a covert radio and modified to hide a wide variety of non-standard weapons and Japanese photographic equipment. Two British Army sergeants known to Dubois – both in civilian clothes – were leaning against the side of the car, smoking cigarettes. They straightened up when Dubois and Cranfield approached, though neither man saluted.

'Sergeant Blake,' Dubois said, nodding by way of welcome. 'Sergeant Harris.' He nodded in the direction of Cranfield. 'This is Lieutenant Cranfield of the SAS, in charge of this mission.'

Both men nodded at Cranfield, neither saying a word.

'You've been briefed?' Cranfield asked.

'Yes, sir,' Sergeant Harris said. 'We're not bringing him back. It's terminal. He stays where he lies.'

'Correct,' Cranfield said. 'So let's get going.'

Sergeant Harris was the driver, with Cranfield sitting in the front beside him. As Dubois took his seat in the back, beside Sergeant Blake, he thought of just how confused were the issues of this conflict and how easily men like Cranfield, even himself, could be driven to taking matters into their own hands, as they were doing right now.

Still, it *had* been a rather bad year: the humiliating fall of the Tory government; the creation of a non-elected, supposedly neutral power-sharing executive to replace direct rule of Ulster from London; the collapse of that executive under the intimidation of the Ulster Workers' strike and IRA violence, including the horrendous Birmingham pub massacre; the Dublin bombing; an IRA truce through Christmas and New Year of 1974–5, and finally the collapse of that truce. Now the SAS was being officially brought in, hopefully to succeed

22

where the regular Army had failed. Dubois was mildly offended.

Sergeant Harris started the car and headed away from the motor pool, driving past rows of Saracen armoured cars, troop trucks, tanks, as well as other Q cars, most of which were visibly well used. The road led around to where the Lynx, Wessex and Army Westland Scout helicopters were taking off and landing, carrying men to and from the many OPs, observation posts, scattered on the high, green hills of the province and manned night and day by rotating, regular army surveillance teams. It was a reminder to Dubois of just how much this little war in Northern Ireland was costing the British public in manpower and money.

'I still don't see why they had to bring in the SAS,' he said distractedly as the Q car approached the heavily guarded main gate. 'I mean, every Army unit in the province has Close Observation Platoons specially trained for undercover operations – so why an official, full complement of SAS?'

'The main problem with your COPS,' Cranfield replied, meaning the Close Observation Platoons, 'is that the men simply can't pass themselves off as Irishmen, and have, in fact, often got into trouble when trying to. Since our men are specially trained for covert operations, they can act as watchers without coming on with the blarney and buying themselves an early grave.'

There was more to it than that, as Dubois knew

from his Whitehall contacts. The decision to send the SAS contingent had been taken by Edward Heath's government as long ago as January 1974. The minority Labour government elected six weeks later – Harold Wilson's second administration – was *not* informed when elements of B Squadron 22 SAS were first deployed to Northern Ireland at that time.

Unfortunately, on 26 January 1974, a former UDR soldier named William Black was shot and seriously wounded by security forces using a silenced sub-machine-gun. When Black was awarded damages, the SAS came under suspicion. The soldiers, not trained for an urban anti-terrorist role and fresh from the Omani desert, had not been made aware of the legal hazards of their new environment.

Worse was to come. B Squadron's contingent was withdrawn abruptly from Ireland after two of its members attempted to rob a bank in Londonderry. Both men were later sentenced to six years' imprisonment, though their just punishment hardly helped the image of the SAS, which was being viewed by many as a secret army of assassins, not much better than the notorious Black and Tans of old. Perhaps for this reason, the presence of the SAS in Ireland during that period was always officially denied.

Nevertheless, when Dubois had first arrived in the province to serve with 4 Field Survey Troop, he found himself inheriting SAS Lieutenant Randolph 'Randy' Cranfield as his deputy, or second-in-command. At first, Dubois and Cranfield had merely visited Intelligence officers in the Armagh area, including 'Major Fred' in Portadown, lying that they were under the direct orders of SIS (MI6) and Army HQ Intelligence staff. When believed by the naïve, they asked for suggestions of worthwhile intelligence targets. This led them to make illicit expeditions across the border, initially just for surveillance, then to 'snatch' IRA members and return them at gunpoint to Northern Ireland to be 'captured' by the RUC and handed over for trial in the north. Now they were going far beyond that – and it had Dubois worried.

'At least your lot have finally been committed *publicly* to Northern Ireland,' he said to Cranfield as the car passed between the heavily fortified sangars on both sides of the electronically controlled gates. 'That might be a help.' 'It's no more than a public relations campaign by the Prime Minister,' Cranfield said with his customary cynicism as the car passed through the gates, which then closed automatically.

'Paddy Devlin's already described it as a cosmetic exercise, pointing out, accurately, that the SAS have always been here.'

That was true enough, Dubois acknowledged to himself. Right or wrong, the recent decision to publicly commit the SAS to Northern Ireland had been imposed by the Prime Minister without warning, even bypassing the Ministry of Defence. Indeed, as Dubois had learnt from friends, Home Secretary Merlyn Rees had already secretly confessed that it was a 'presentational thing', a melodramatic way of letting the public know that the most legendary group of soldiers in the history of British warfare were about to descend on Northern Ireland and put paid to the IRA.

'What the Downing Street announcement *really* signalled,' Dubois said, still trying to forget his nervousness, 'was a change in the SAS role from intelligence gathering to combat.'

'Right,' Cranfield replied. 'So don't feel too bad about what we're doing. Just think of it as legitimate combat. You'll sleep easier that way.'

'I hope so,' Dubois said.

As the gates clanged shut behind the Q car, Sergeant Harris turned onto the road leading to the border, which was only a few miles from the camp. Once the grim, high walls of corrugated iron were out of sight, the rolling green hills came into view, reminding Dubois of how beautiful Northern Ireland was, how peaceful it always looked, away from the trouble spots.

This illusion of peace was rudely broken when his observant eye picked out the many overt OPs scattered about the hills, with high-powered binoculars and telescopes glinting under makeshift roofs of camouflaged netting and turf, constantly surveying the roads and fields. It was also broken when armoured trucks and tanks, bristling with weapons, trundled along the road, travelling between the border and the army camp.

After driving for about ten minutes they came to the British Army roadblock located two miles before the border. Sergeant Harris stopped to allow the soldiers, all wearing full OGs, with helmets and chin straps, and armed with SA-80 assanlt rifles, to show their papers. Presenting their real papers, as distinct from the false documents they were also carrying for use inside the Republic, they were waved on and soon reached the border. To avoid the Gardai — the police force of the Republic of Ireland — they took an unmarked side road just before the next village and kept going until they were safely over the border. Ten minutes later they came to a halt in the shady lane that led up to O'Halloran's conveniently isolated farmhouse.

'He can't see us or hear from here,' Cranfield said, 'and we're going the rest of the way by foot. You wait here in the car, Sergeant Harris. No one's likely to come along here, except, perhaps, for some innocent local like the postman or milkman.'

'And if he does?'

'We can't afford to have witnesses.'

'Right, sir. Terminate.'

Cranfield glanced back over his shoulder at Captain Dubois, still in the rear seat. 'Are you ready?'

'Yes.'

'Good, let's go. You too, Sergeant Blake.'

Cranfield and Dubois unholstered their 9mm Browning High Power handguns as they got out of the car. Sergeant Blake withdrew a silenced L34A1 Sterling sub-machine-gun from a hidden panel beneath his feet and unfolded the stock as he climbed out of the car to stand beside the other two men. After releasing their safety-catches, the men walked up the lane, away from the Q car, until they arrived at the wooden gate that led into the fields surrounding the farmhouse.

It was not yet 8.30 a.m. and the sun was still trying to break through a thick layer of cloud, casting shadows over the misty green hills on all sides of the house. Birds were singing. The wind was moaning slightly. Smoke was rising from the chimney in the thatched roof, indicating that O'Halloran, known to live alone, was up and about.

His two Alsatians, tethered to a post in the front yard, hadn't noticed the arrival of the men and were sleeping contentedly. The slightest sound, however, would awaken them.

Cranfield nodded at Sergeant Blake. The latter set his L34A1 to semi-automatic fire, leaned slightly forward with his right leg taking his weight and the left giving him balance, then pressed the extended stock of the weapon into his shoulder with his body leaning into the gun. He released the cocking handle, raised the rear assembly sight, then took careful aim. He fired two short bursts, moving the barrel right for the second burst, his body shaking slightly from the backblast. Loose soil spat up violently, silently, around the sleeping dogs, making them shudder, obscuring the flying bone and geyzering blood from their exploding heads. When the spiralling dust had settled down, the heads of the dogs resembled pomegranates. Blake's silenced L34A1 had made practically no sound and the dogs had died too quickly even to yelp.

Using a hand signal, Cranfield indicated that the men should slip around the gate posts rather than open the chained gate, then cross the ground in front of the farmhouse. This they did, moving as quietly as possible, spreading out as they advanced with their handguns at the ready, merely glancing in a cursory manner at the Alsatians now lying in pools of blood.

When they reached the farmhouse, Cranfield nodded at Sergeant Blake, who returned the nod, then slipped quietly around the side of the house to cover the back door. When he had disappeared around the back, Cranfield and Dubois took up positions on either side of the door, holding their pistols firmly, applying equal pressure between the thumb and fingers of the firing hand.

Cranfield was standing upright, his back pressed to the wall. Dubois was on one knee, already aiming his pistol at the door. When the latter nodded,

Cranfield spun around, kicked the door open and rushed in, covered by Dubois.

O'Halloran was sitting in his pyjamas at the kitchen table, about ten feet away, as the door was torn from its hinges and crashed to the floor. Shocked, he looked up from his plate, the fork still to his mouth, as Cranfield rushed in, stopped, spread his legs wide, and prepared to fire the gun two-handed.

'This is for Phillips,' Cranfield said, then fired the first shot.

O'Halloran jerked convulsively and slapped his free hand on the table, his blood already spurting over the bacon and eggs as his fork fell, clattering noisily on the tiles. He jerked again with the second bullet. Trying to stand, he twisted backwards, his chair buckling and breaking beneath him as he crashed to the floor.

Dubois came in after Cranfield, crouched low, aiming left and right, covering the room as Cranfield emptied his magazine, one shot after another in the classic 'double tap', though using all thirteen bullets instead of two.

O'Halloran, already dead, was jerking spasmodically from each bullet as Sergeant Blake, hearing the shots, kicked the back door in and rushed through the house, checking each room as he went, prepared to cut down anything that moved, but finding nothing at all. By the time he reached the kitchen at the front, the double tap was completed.

Sergeant Blake glanced at the dead man on the floor. 'Good job, boss,' he commented quietly.

'Let's go,' Dubois said.

Cranfield knelt beside O'Halloran, placed his fingers on his neck, checked that he was dead, then stood up again.

'Day's work done,' he said.

Unable to return Cranfield's satisfied grin, though feeling relieved, Captain Dubois just nodded and led the three men out of the house. They returned to the Q car, not glancing back once, and let Sergeant Harris drive them away, back to Northern Ireland.

2

Martin was leaning on the rusty railing when the ship that had brought him and the others from Liverpool inched into Belfast harbour in the early hours of the morning. His hair was longer than it should have been, windswept, dishevelled. He was wearing a roll-necked sweater, a bomber jacket, blue jeans and a pair of old suede boots, and carrying a small shoulder bag. The others, he knew, looked the same, though they were now in the bar, warming up with mugs of tea.

Looking at the lights beaming over the dark, dismal harbour, he was reminded of the brilliant light that had temporarily blinded him when the Directing Staff conducting the brutal Resistance to Interrogation (RTI) exercises had whipped the hood off his head. Later they had congratulated him on having passed that final hurdle even before his eyes had readjusted to the light in the bare, cell-like room in the Joint Services Interrogation Unit of 22 SAS Training Wing, Hereford. Even as he was being led from the room, knowing he would soon be bound for the last stages of his Continuation Training in Borneo, he had seen another young man, Corporal Wigan of the Light Infantry, being escorted out of the building with tears in his eyes.

'He was the one you shared the truck with,' his Director of Training had told him, 'but he finally cracked, forgot where he was, and told us everything we wanted to know. Now he's being RTU'd.'

Being returned to your unit of origin was doubly humiliating, first through the failure to get into the SAS, then through having to face your old mates, who would know you had failed. Even now, thinking of how easily it could have happened to him, Martin, formerly of the Royal Engineers, practically shuddered at the thought of it.

Feeling cold and dispirited by the sight of the bleak docks of Belfast, he hurried back into the bar where the other men, some recently badged like him, others old hands who had last fought in Oman, all of them in civilian clothing, were sipping hot tea and pretending to be normal passengers.

Sergeant Frank Lampton, who had been Martin's Director of Training during the horrors of Continuation Training, was leaning back in his chair, wearing a thick overcoat, corduroy trousers, a tatty shirt buttoned at the neck, a V-necked sweater and badly scuffed suede shoes. With his blond hair dishevelled and his clothing all different sizes, as if picked up in charity shops, he did not look remotely like the slim, fit, slightly glamorous figure who had been Martin's DT.

Sitting beside Sergeant Lampton was Corporal Phil Ricketts. Their strong friendship had been forged in the fierce fighting of the 'secret' war in Dhofar, Oman, in 1972. Ricketts was a pleasant, essentially serious man with a wife and child in Wood Green, North London. He didn't talk about them much, but when he did it was with real pride and love. Unlike the sharp-tongued, ferret-faced Trooper 'Gumboot' Gillis, sitting opposite.

Badged with Ricketts just before going to Dhofar, Gumboot hailed from Barnstaple, Devon, where he had a wife, Linda, whom he seemed to hold in less than high esteem. 'I was in Belfast before,' he'd explained to Martin a few nights earlier, 'but with 3 Para. When I returned home, that bitch had packed up and left with the kids. That's why, when I was badged and sent back here, I was pleased as piss. I'll take a Falls Road hag any day. At least you know where you stand with them.'

'Up against an alley wall,' Jock McGregor said.

Corporal McGregor had been shot through the hand in Oman and looked like the tough nut he was. Others who had fought with Lampton, Ricketts and Gumboot in Oman had gone their separate ways, with the big black poet, Trooper Andrew Winston, being returned there in 1975. A lot of the men had joked that the reason Andrew had been transferred to another squadron and sent back to Oman was that his black face couldn't possibly pass for a Paddy's. Whatever the true cause, he had been awarded for bravery during the SAS strikes against rebel strongholds in Defa and Shershitti.

Sitting beside Jock was Trooper Danny 'Baby Face' Porter, from Kingswinford, in the West Midlands. He was as quiet as a mouse and, though nicknamed 'Baby Face' because of his innocent, wide-eyed, choirboy appearance, was said to have been one of the most impressive of all the troopers who had recently been badged — a natural soldier who appeared to fear nothing and was ferociously competent with weapons. His speciality was the 'double tap' — thirteen rounds discharged from a Browning High Power handgun in under three seconds, at close range — which some had whispered might turn out useful in the mean streets of Belfast.

Not as quiet as Danny, but also just badged and clearly self-conscious with the more experienced troopers, Hugh 'Taff' Burgess was a broad-chested Welshman with a dark, distant gaze, a sweet, almost childlike nature and, reportedly, a violent temper when aroused or drunk. Throughout the whole SAS Selection and Training course Taff had been slightly slow in learning, very thorough at everything, helpful and encouraging to others, and always even-tempered. True, he had wrecked a few pubs in Hereford, but while in the SAS barracks in the town he had been a dream of good humour and generosity. Not ambitious, and not one to shine too brightly, he was, nevertheless, a good soldier, popular with everyone.

Last but not least was Sergeant 'Dead-eye Dick' Parker, who didn't talk much. Rumour had it that he had been turned into a withdrawn, ruthless fighting machine by his terrible experience in the Telok Anson swamp in Malaya in 1958. According to the eye-witness accounts of other Omani veterans such as Sergeant Ricketts and Gumboot, Parker, when in Oman with them, had worn Arab clothing and fraternized mostly with the unpredictable, violent firqats, Dhofaris who had renounced their communist comrades and lent their support to the Sultan. Now, lounging lazily on a chair in blue denims and a tatty old ski jacket, he looked like any other middle-aged man running slightly to seed. Only his grey gaze, cold and ever shifting, revealed that he was alert and still potentially lethal.

The men were scattered all around the lounge, not speaking, pretending not to know one another. When the boat docked and the passengers started disembarking, they shuffled out of the lounge with them, but remained well back or took up positions on the open deck, waiting for the last of the passengers to disembark.

Looking in both directions along the quayside,

Martin saw nothing moving among the gangplanks tilted on end, scattered railway sleepers and coils of thick mooring cables. The harbour walls rose out of the filthy black water, stained a dirty brown by years of salt water and the elements, supporting an ugly collection of warehouses, huts, tanks and prefabricated administration buildings. Unmanned cranes loomed over the water, their hooks swinging slightly in the wind blowing in from the sea. Out in the harbour, green and red pilot lights floated on a gentle sea. Seagulls circled overhead, crying keenly, in the grey light of morning.

Having previously been told to wait on the deck until their driver beckoned to them, the men did so. The last of the other passengers had disembarked when Martin, glancing beyond the quayside, saw a green minibus leaving its position in the car park. It moved between rows of empty cars and the trailers of articulated lorries, eventually leaving the car park through gates guarded by RUC guards wearing flak jackets and armed with 5.56mm Ruger Mini-14 assault rifles. When the minibus reached the quayside and stopped by the empty gangplank, Martin knew that it had to be their transport.

As the driver, also wearing civilian clothing, got out of his car, Sergeant Lampton made his way down the gangplank and spoke to him. The man nodded affirmatively. A group of armed RUC guards emerged from one of the prefabricated huts along the quayside to stand guard while the men's bergen rucksacks were unloaded and heaped up on the quayside. There were no weapons; these would be obtained from the armoury in the camp they were going to. All of the men were, however, already armed with 9mm Browning High Power handguns, which they were wearing in cross-draw holsters under their jackets.

When the last of the bergens had been unloaded, Lampton turned back and waved the men down to the quayside. Martin went down between Ricketts and Gumboot, following the first into the back of the minibus, where a lot of the men were already seated. Gumboot was the last to get in. When he did so, one of the RUC guards slid the door shut and the driver took off, heading out into the mean streets of Belfast.

'Can we talk at last?' Gumboot asked. 'I can't stand this silence.'

'Gumboot wants to talk,' Jock McGregor said. 'God help us all.'

'He's talking already,' Ricketts said. 'I distinctly heard him. Like a little mouse squeaking.'

'Ha, ha. Merely attempting to break the silence, boss,' retorted Gumboot, 'and keep us awake until we basha down. That boat journey seemed endless.'

'You won't get to basha down until tonight, so you better keep talking.'

'Don't encourage him,' Jock said. 'It's too early to have to listen to his bullshit. I've got a headache already.'

'It's the strain of trying to think,' Gumboot informed him. 'You're not used to it, Jock.'

His gaze moved to the window and the dismal streets beyond, where signs saying NO SUR-RENDER! and SMASH SINN FEIN! fought for attention with enormous, angry paintings on the walls of buildings, showing the customary propa-ganda of civil war: clenched fists, hooded men clasping weapons, the various insignia of the paramilitary groups on both sides of the divide, those in Shankill, the Falls Road, and the grim, ghettoized housing estates of West Belfast.

'How anyone can imagine this place worth all the slaughter,' Taff Burgess said, studying the grim, wet, barricaded streets, 'I just can't imagine.'

'They don't think it's worth it.' Jock said. 'They're just a bunch of thick Paddies and mur-derous bastards using any excuse.'

'Not quite true,' Martin said. Brought up by strictly methodist parents in Swindon, not religious himself, but highly conscious of right and wrong, he had carefully read up on Ireland before coming here and was shocked by what he had learnt. 'These people have hatreds that go back to 1601,' he explained, 'when the Catholic barons were defeated and Protestants from England arrived by boat to begin colonization and genocide.'

'1601!' Gumboot said in disgust. 'The Paddies sure have fucking long memories.'

'The Catholics were thrown out of their own

land,' Martin continued, feeling a little self-conscious. 'When they returned to attack the Protestants with pitchforks and stones, the British hanged and beheaded thousands of them. Some were tarred with pitch and dynamite, then set on fire.'

'Ouch!' Taff exclaimed.

'When the Catholics were broken completely,' Martin continued in a trance of historical recollection, 'their religion was outlawed, their language was forbidden, and they became untouchables who lived in the bogs below the Protestant towns. They endured that for a couple of hundred years.'

'You're still talking about centuries ago,' Gumboot said. 'That's a long time to hold those old grudges. Might as well go back to the garden of Eden and complain that you weren't given a bite of the fucking apple.'

'It's not the same thing,' Martin insisted, feeling embarrassed that he was talking so much, but determined to get his point across. 'We're not talking about something that happened just once, centuries ago, but about something that's never really stopped.'

'So the poor buggers were thrown out of their homes and into the bogs,' Taff Burgess said with genuine sympathy, his brown gaze focused inward. 'So what happened next, then?'

'Over the centuries, Belfast became a wealthy industrial centre, dominated entirely by Protestants.

But the Catholics started returning to the city about 1800, and naturally, as they were still being treated like scum, they were resentful and struck back.'

'Nothing like a bit of the old "ultra-violence" to get out your frustrations,' said Gumboot, grinning wickedly. 'Remember that film, *A Clockwork Orange*? Fucking good, that was.'

'Race riots and pogroms became commonplace,' Martin continued, now getting into his stride. 'It burst out every five or six years, eventually leading to the formation of Catholic and Protestant militia. Civil war erupted in 1920. In 1921 the country was partitioned, with the six provinces of the North becoming a British statelet, ruled by its Protestant majority.'

'Big fucking deal,' Gumboot said as the minibus passed through a street of small terraced houses, many with their windows and doorways bricked up. Here the signs said: PROVOS RULE! and BRITS OUT! Even at this early hour of the morning there were gangs of scruffy youths on the street corners, looking for trouble. 'What was so bad about that?'

'Well, Catholics couldn't get jobs and their slums became worse,' Martin explained. 'The electoral laws were manipulated to favour owners of property, who were mostly Protestants. Even after more riots in the thirties and forties, nothing changed. Finally, in 1969, the Catholics took to the streets again, where they were attacked by Protestant police and vigilantes. This time they refused to lie down and the whole city went up in flames.'

'I remember that well,' Jock said. 'I saw it on TV. Mobs all over the place, thousands fleeing from their homes, and Army tanks in the streets. I could hardly believe what I was seeing. A civil war on British soil!'

'Right,' Ricketts chipped in. 'And by the time they were done, you had Catholics on one side, Protestants on the other, and the British equivalent of the Berlin Wall between.'

He pointed out of the window of the van, where they could see the actual 'Peace Line': a fifteen-foot-high wall topped with iron spikes, cutting across roads, through rows of houses, and, as they had all been informed, right across the city.

'Which led,' Sergeant Lampton added laconically, 'to the birth of the masked IRA terrorist and his opposite number, the loyalist terrorist in balaclava.'

'And here we are, caught in the middle,' Ricketts said, 'trying to keep the peace.'

'Trying to stay alive,' Gumboot corrected him, 'which is all it comes down to. I've only got one aim in this piss-hole – to make sure that none of the bastards on either side puts one in my back. Fuck all the rest of it.'

The minibus was now leaving the city to travel along the M1, through rolling hills which, Martin noticed, were dotted with British Army observation posts. Even as he saw the distant OPs, an AH-7 Lynx helicopter was hovering over one of them to insert replacements and take off the men already there. The OPs, Martin knew, were resupplied with men and equipment only by air – never by road.

'Hard to believe that's a killing ground out there,' Sergeant Lampton said. 'If it wasn't for the OPs on the hills, it would all seem so peaceful.'

'It looked peaceful in Oman as well,' Ricketts said, 'until the *Adoo* appeared. It's the same with those hills – except instead of *Adoo* snipers, you have the terrorists. They look pretty serene from down here, but you're right – those are killing fields.'

Martin felt an odd disbelief as he looked at the lush, serene hills and thought of how many times they had been used to hide torture and murder. That feeling remained with him when the minibus turned off the motorway and made its way along a winding narrow lane to the picturesque village of Bessbrook, where the British army had taken over the old mill. Located only four miles from the border, it was a village with a strongly Protestant, God-fearing community – there was not a single pub – and it was presently living through a grim spate of sectarian killings.

As revenge for the killing by Protestant terrorists of five local Catholics, a splinter group calling itself the South Armagh Republican Action Force had stopped a local bus and gunned down eleven men, most of them from Bessbrook, who were on their way home after work. Only one passenger and the Catholic driver had survived. Since that atrocity, both Protestant and Catholic 'death squads' had been stalking the countryside of south Armagh, killing people wholesale. It was this, Martin believed, that had prompted the British government to publicly commit the SAS to the area. Yet now, as the minibus passed through the guarded gates of the old mill, he could scarcely believe that this pretty village was at the heart of so many murderous activities.

'OK,' Sergeant Lampton said when the minibus braked to a halt inside the grounds of the mill. 'The fun's over. All out.'

The side door of the vehicle slid open and they all climbed out into the Security Forces (SF) base as the electronically controlled gates whined shut behind them. The mill had been turned into a grim compound surrounded by high corrugated-iron walls topped by barbed wire. The protective walls were broken up with a series of regularly placed concrete sentry boxes under sandbagged roofs and camouflaged netting. An ugly collection of Portakabins was being used for accommodation and administration. RUC policemen, again wearing flak jackets and carrying Ruger assault rifles, mingled with regular Army soldiers. Saracen armoured cars and tanks were lined up in rows by the side of the motor pool. Closed-circuit TV cameras showed

44

the duty operator in the operations room precisely who was coming or going through the main gates between the heavily fortified sangars.

'Looks like a fucking prison,' Gumboot complained.

'Home sweet home,' Sergeant Lampton said.

3

'Settle down, men,' Lieutenant Cranfield said when he had taken his place on the small platform in the briefing room, beside Captain Dubois and an Army sergeant seated at a desk piled high with manila folders. When his new arrivals had quietened down, Cranfield continued: 'You men are here on attachment to 14 Intelligence Company, an intelligence unit that replaced the Military Reconnaissance Force, or MRF, of Brigadier Kitson, who was Commander of Land Forces, Northern Ireland, from 1970 to 1972. A little background information is therefore necessary.'

Some of the men groaned mockingly; others rolled their eyes. Grinning, Cranfield let them grumble for a moment, meanwhile letting his gaze settle briefly on familiar faces: Sergeants Lampton, Ricketts and Parker, as well as Corporal Jock McGregor and Troopers 'Gumboot' Gillis and Danny 'Baby Face' Porter, all of whom had fought bravely in Oman, before returning to act as Directing Staff at 22 SAS Training Wing,

Hereford. There were also some recently badged new men whom he would check out later.

'In March 1972,' Cranfield at last began, 'shortly after the Stormont Parliament was discontinued and direct rule from Westminster substituted, selected members of the SAS, mainly officers, were posted here as individuals to sensitive jobs in Military Intelligence, attached to units already serving in the province. Invariably, they found themselves in a world of petty, often lethal jealousies and division among conflicting agencies – a world of dirty tricks instigated by Military Intelligence officers and their superiors. The MRF was just one of those agencies, causing its own share of problems.'

Now Cranfield glanced at the newcomer, Martin Renshaw, who had endured Sergeant Lampton's perfect impersonation of an Irish terrorist during the horrendous final hours of the RTI exercises during Continuation Training. What was more, he had done so without forgetting that it was only an exercise, unlike so many others, who were RTU'd as a result. According to his report, Renshaw was a serious young man with good technological training, pedantic tendencies, and heady ambitions.

'As some of you have come straight from Oman,' Cranfield continued, 'it's perhaps worth pointing out that certain members of the MRF were, like the firqats of Dhofar, former enemies who had been turned. Occasionally using these IRA renegades – known as "Freds" – as spotters, the

MRF's Q-car patrols identified many active IRA men and women, sometimes photographing them with cameras concealed in the boot of the car. Too often, however, MRF operations went over the top, achieving nothing but propaganda for the IRA.'

'Just like the green slime,' Gumboot said, copping some laughs from his mates and, as Cranfield noticed, a stony glance from his uneasy associate, the Army intelligence officer Captain Dubois.

'Very funny, Trooper Gillis,' Cranfield said. 'Perhaps you'd like to step up here and take over.'

'No, thanks, boss. Please continue.'

Cranfield nodded, secretly admiring Gumboot's impertinence, which he viewed as a virtue not possessed by soldiers of the regular Army. 'In 1972 a couple of embarrassing episodes led to the disbandment of Kitson's organization. Number one was when a two-man team opened fire with a Thompson sub-machine-gun from a moving car on men standing at a Belfast bus stop. Though both soldiers were prosecuted, they claimed they'd been fired at first. The second was when the IRA assassinated the driver of an apparently innocuous laundry van in Belfast. This led to the revelation that the company that owned the van, the so-called Four Square Laundry, was actually an MRF front, collecting clothing in suspect districts for forensic examination.'

'Proper dirty laundry,' Jock McGregor said, winning a few more laughs.

'Yes,' Cranfield said, 'it was that all right. Anyway, those two incidents caused a stir and brought an end to the MRF, which was disbanded early in 1973. But it soon became apparent that as the police, whether in or out of uniform, were soft targets for gunmen, a viable substitute for the MRF was required. This would require men who could penetrate the republican ghettos unnoticed, and who possessed keen powers of observation, quick wits, and even quicker trigger fingers.'

'That's us!' the normally quiet Danny Porter, 'Baby Face', said with a shy grin.

'Not at that time,' Cranfield replied, 'though certainly the training officer for the new team was then serving with 22 SAS. In fact, the new unit, formed at the end of 1973, was 14 Intelligence Company. While it was the job of that company to watch and gather information about the IRA, the SAS's function was to act on the intelligence supplied by them and take action when necessary.'

'Excuse me, boss,' Taff Burgess asked, putting his hand in the air like an eager schoolboy. 'Are you saying that 14 Intelligence Company never gets involved in overt action against the IRA? That they've never had, or caused, casualties?'

'No. They have suffered, and have caused, casualties – but only when spotted and usually only when the terrorist has fired first. Their function is to gather intelligence – not to physically engage the enemy. That's our job. To do it within the law, however, we have to know exactly who and what we're involved with here in the province.'

Cranfield nodded at the Army sergeant standing beside the intelligence officer. The sergeant started distributing his manila folders to the SAS troopers sitting in the chairs. 'The information I'm about to give you,' Cranfield said, 'is contained in more detail in those folders. I want you to read it later and memorize it. For now, I'll just summarize the main points.'

He paused until his assistant, Sergeant Lovelock, had given out the last of the folders and returned to his desk.

'At present there are fourteen British Army battalions in Northern Ireland, each with approximately 650 men, each unit deployed in its own Tactical Area of Responsibility, or TAOR, known as a "patch". As the RUC's B Special Reserve were highly suspect in the eyes of the Republicans, their responsibilities have been handed over to the Ulster Defence Regiment, a reserve unit composed in the main of local part-timers. Unfortunately the UDR is already deeply unpopular with the Catholics, who view its members as hard-line loyalists. Most Army commanders are no more impressed by the UDR, believing, like me, that it's dangerous to let part-time Protestant reservists into hard Republican areas.'

'Are they reliable otherwise?' Ricketts asked.

'Many of us feel that the Royal Ulster Constabulary is more reliable than the UDR, though we certainly don't believe policemen are capable of taking complete charge of security. This is evidenced by the fact that RUC officers often refuse to accompany the Army on missions – either because they think it's too risky or because they feel that their presence would antagonize the locals even more than the Army does.'

'That sounds bloody helpful,' Jock McGregor said sourly.

'Quite. In fact, in strongly Republican areas the RUC have virtually ceded authority to us. They do, however, have two very important departments: the Criminal Investigations Department, or CID, in charge of interrogating suspects and gathering evidence after major incidents; and the Special Branch, or SB, which runs the informer networks vital to us all. They also have a Special Patrol Group, or SPG, with mobile anti-terrorist squads trained in the use of firearms and riot control. We can call upon them when necessary.'

'What about the police stations?' Lampton asked.

'Sixteen divisions – rather like Army battalions – in total. Some are grouped into each of three specific regions – Belfast, South and North – each with an assistant chief constable in charge, with as much authority as the Army's three brigadiers. Those three chief constables report in turn to the chief constable at RUC HQ at Knock, east Belfast.'

'Who calls the shots?' Jock McGregor asked.

'The regular Army and UDR battalions are divided between three brigade HQs – 29 Brigade in the Belfast area, 8 Brigade in Londonderry and 3 Brigade in Portadown, the latter responsible for covering the border. The Brigade Commanders report to the Commander Land Forces, or CLF, at Lisburn, the top Army man in Ulster. He has to answer to the General Officer Command-ing, or GOC, who, though an Army officer, is also in charge of the RAF and Royal Navy detachments in the province. He's also responsible for co-ordination with the police and ministers. The HQNI, or Headquarters Northern Ireland, is located in barracks at Lisburn, a largely Protestant town just outside Belfast that includes the HQ of 39 brigade. Regarding the role of 14 Intelligence Company in all this, I'll hand you over to Captain Dubois.'

Slightly nervous about talking to a bunch of men who would feel resentful about working with the regular Army, Captain Dubois coughed into his fist before commencing.

'Good morning, gentlemen.' When most of the Troop just stared steadily at him, deliberately trying to unnerve him, he continued quickly: 'Like the SAS, 14 Intelligence Company is formed from soldiers who volunteer from other units and have to pass a stiff selection test. It recruits from the Royal Marines as well as the Army, though it looks for resourcefulness and the ability to bear the strain of long-term surveillance, rather than the physical stamina required for the Special Air Service.'

Applause, cheers and hoots of derision alike greeted Dubois' words. Still not used to the informality of the SAS, he glanced uncertainly at Cranfield, who grinned at him, amused by his nervousness.

'The unit has one detachment with each of the three brigades in Ulster,' Dubois continued. 'Each consists of twenty soldiers under the command of a captain. We operate under a variety of cover names, including the Northern Ireland Training Advisory Team, or NITAT, and the Intelligence and Security Group, or Int and Sy Group. Like the original MRF, most of our work involves setting up static OPs or the observation of suspected or known terrorists from unmarked Q cars. These have covert radios and concealed compartments for other weapons and photographic equipment. Most of the static OPs in Belfast are manned by our men and located in both Republican and Loyalist areas, such as Shankill, the Falls Road and West Belfast's Turf Lodge and the Creggan. You men will be used mainly for OPs in rural areas and observation and other actions in Q cars here in Belfast. You will, in effect, be part of 14 Intelligence Company, doing that kind of work, initially under our supervision, then on your own.'

'Armed?' Danny Porter asked quietly.

'Yes. With weapons small enough to be concealed. These include the 9mm Browning High Power handgun and, in certain circumstances, small sub-machine-guns.'

'What's our brief regarding their use?'

'Your job is observation, not engagement, though the latter isn't always avoidable. Bear in mind that you won't be able to pass yourselves off as locals, eavesdropping in Republican bars or clubs. Try it and you'll soon attract the curiosity of IRA sympathizers, some as young as fourteen, looking as innocent as new-born babies, but almost certainly in the IRA youth wing. If one of those innocents speaks to you, you can rest assured that he'll soon be followed by a hard man of more mature years. Shortly after the hard man comes the coroner.'

Thankfully, the men laughed at Dubois' sardonic remark, encouraging him to continue in a slightly more relaxed manner.

'For that reason we recommend that you don't leave your Q car unless absolutely necessary. We also recommend that you don't try using an Irish accent. If you're challenged, say no more than: "Fuck off!" And say it with conviction.' When the men laughed again, Dubois said: 'I know it sounds funny, but it's actually the only phrase that might work. Otherwise, you cut out of there.'

'At what point do we use our weapons?' the new man, Martin Renshaw, boldly asked.

'When you feel that your life is endangered and there's no time to make your escape.'

'Do we shoot to kill?' 'Baby Face' asked.

'Shooting to wound is a risky endeavour that rarely stops a potential assassin,' Lieutenant Cranfield put in. 'You shoot to stop the man coming at you, which means you can't take any chances. Your aim is to down him.'

'Which means the heart.'

'Yes, Trooper.'

'Is there actually a shoot-to-kill policy?' Ricketts asked.

Captain Dubois smiled tightly. 'Categorically not. Let's say, instead, that there's a contingency policy which covers a fairly broad range of options. I should remind you, however, that the IRA don't always display our restraint. London's policy of minimum fire-power, rejecting the use of ground- or air-launched missiles, mines, heavy machine-guns and armour, has contained the casualty figures to a level which no other government fighting a terrorist movement has been able to match. On the other hand, the Provisional IRA alone presently has at least 1200 active members and they've been well equipped by American sympathizers with a few hundred fully automatic 5.6mm Armalites and 7.62mm M60 machine-guns, as well as heavier weapons, such as the Russian-made RPG 7 short-range anti-tank weapon with rocket-propelled grenades. So let's say we have reasonable cause to believe in reasonable force.'

'Does reasonable force include the taking out of former IRA commanders?' Sergeant 'Dead-eye Dick' Parker asked abruptly.

'Pardon?' Dubois asked, looking as shocked as Cranfield suddenly felt.

'I'm referring to the fact that a few days ago a former IRA commander, Shaun O'Halloran, was taken out by an unknown assassin, or assassins, while sitting in his own home in the Irish Republic.'

Already knowing that his assassination of O'Halloran had rocked the intelligence community, as well as outraging the IRA, but not aware before now that it had travelled all the way back to Hereford, Cranfield glanced at Dubois, took note of his flushed cheeks, and decided to go on the attack.

'Are you suggesting that the SAS or 14 Intelligence Company had something to do with that?' he addressed Parker, feigning disbelief.

Parker, however, was not intimidated. 'I'm not suggesting anything, boss,' he replied in his soft-voiced manner. 'I'm merely asking if such an act would be included under reasonable force?'

'No,' Captain Dubois intervened, trying to gather his wits together and take control of the situation.

'I deny that categorically. And as you said, the assassin was unknown.'

'The IRA are claiming it was the work of the SAS.'

'The IRA blame us for a lot of things,' Cranfield put in, aware that Parker was not a man to fool with.

'Is it true,' Ricketts asked, 'that they also blame the SAS for certain actions taken by 14 Intelligence Company?'

When he saw Dubois glance uneasily at him, Cranfield deliberately covered his own temporary nervousness by smiling as casually as possible at Ricketts, who was, he knew, as formidable a soldier as Parker. 'Yes,' he said, 'that's true. It's a natural mistake to make. They know we're involved in surveillance, so that makes us suspect.'

'Who do you think was responsible for the assassination of O'Halloran?'

The questioner was Sergeant Parker again, studying Dubois with his steady, emotionless gaze. Dubois reddened and became more visibly flustered until rescued by Cranfield, who said: 'O'Halloran's assassination wasn't in keeping with the psychological tactics employed by the Regiment in Malaya and Oman. More likely, then, it was committed by one of the paramilitary groups – possibly even the product of internal conflict between warring IRA factions. It certainly wasn't an example of what the SAS – or 14

Intelligence Company — means by "reasonable force".'

'But the IRA,' Parker went on in his quietly relentless way, 'have hinted that O'Halloran may have been involved with a British army undercover agent, Corporal Phillips, who recently committed suicide for unexplained reasons.'

'Corporal Phillips is believed to have been under considerable stress,' Captain Dubois put in quickly, 'which is not unusual in this line of business. May we go on?'

Sergeant Parker stared hard at the officer, but said no more.

'Good,' Dubois went on, determined to kill the subject. 'Perhaps I should point out, regarding this, that while occasionally we may have to resort to physical force, only one in seven of the 1800 people killed in the Province have died at the hands of the security forces, which total around 30,000 men and women at any given time. I think that justifies our use of the phrase "reasonable force".'

Dubois glanced at Lieutenant Cranfield, who stepped forward again.

'We have it on the best of authority that the British government is about to abandon the special category status that's allowed convicted terrorists rights not enjoyed by prisoners anywhere else in the United Kingdom. Under the new rules, loyalist and republican terrorists in the newly built H-blocks at the Maze Prison will be treated as ordinary felons.

The drill parades and other paramilitary trappings that have been permitted in internment camps will no longer be allowed. This is bound to become a major issue in the nationalist community and increase the activities of the IRA. For that reason, I would ask you to remember this. In the past two decades the IRA have killed about 1800 people, including over a hundred citizens of the British mainland, about eight hundred locals, nearly three hundred policemen and 635 soldiers. Make sure you don't personally add to that number.'

He waited until his words had sunk in, then nodded at Captain Dubois.

'Please make your way to the motor pool,' Dubois told the men. 'There you'll find a list containing the name of your driver and the number of your Q car. Your first patrol will be tomorrow morning, just after first light. Be careful. Good luck.'

Still holding their manila folders in their hands, the men filed out of the briefing room, leaving Captain Dubois and Lieutenant Cranfield alone. When the last of the SAS troopers and Sergeant Lovelock had left, Dubois removed a handkerchief from his pocket and wiped sweat from his forehead.

'That was close,' he said. 'Damn it, Cranfield, I knew we shouldn't have done it.'

'Small potatoes,' Cranfield replied, though he didn't feel as confident as he sounded. 'The Irish eat lots of those.'

4

They left the camp at dawn, driving out through the high, corrugated-iron gates, between the two heavily reinforced sangars and, just beyond them, on both sides, the perimeter lights and coils of barbed wire. The gates whined electronically as they opened and shut. The car's exit, Martin knew, was being observed and noted by the guard in the operations room via the closed-circuit TV camera. Even before the gates had closed behind the car, the driver was turning into the narrow country road that would take them on the picturesque, winding, five-mile journey through the morning mist to the M1.

Martin had been very impressed with the previous day's briefing and now, sitting in the rear seat beside Gumboot, he was excited and slightly fearful, even though he had his 9mm Browning High Power handgun in the cross-draw position (in a Len Dixon holster over the rib cage, with four 13-round magazines) and had been shown where the other weapons were concealed.

Also concealed was a Pace Communications Landmaster III hand-held transceiver with a webbing harness, miniature microphone, earphone and encoder, located near the floor between the two front seats; and a 35mm Nikon F-801 camera with a matrix metering system, sophisticated autofocus, electronic rangefinder and long exposure. It was hidden under the Ordnance Survey map of Belfast that was spread for the purpose over Ricketts's lap.

The Q car had been specially adapted to carry a variety of concealed non-standard-issue weapons, including the short, compact Ingram 9mm sub-machine-gun with detachable suppressor and pull-out shoulder-and-hip stock, ideal for anti-terrorist work.

All of the men in the car were wearing the same scruffy civilian clothing that they had worn on the night ferry.

As their driver, Sergeant Lovelock, took the A1, which led all the way to the heart of Republican Belfast, Martin unholstered the Browning and held it on his lap, as he had been instructed, hiding it under a folded newspaper. Nevertheless, he held it at the ready, with his thumb on the safety-catch and his trigger finger resting on the trigger guard.

It was an early morning in January, and there was a heavy layer of frost on the ground, with spikes of ice hanging dramatically from the wintry trees. The windscreen was filthy and frosted over again even as it was wiped clean by the automatic wipers. The motorway ran straight as an arrow between hills covered with grass and gorse, on which cows and sheep roamed, disturbed only by the AH-7 Lynx helicopters rising and falling over the Army OPs.

'The early morning resups,' Sergeant Lovelock explained. 'Men and supplies. Don't fancy static OPs myself, stuck up there for hours, either sweltering in the heat or freezing your nuts off under all that turf and netting. Not my idea of fun.'

'You're the man who gave us the manila folders at the meeting,' Ricketts said.

'You're not blind,' Lovelock replied.

'You prefer being in a Q car?' Ricketts asked him.

'That's for sure. I like being able to move around instead of just waiting for something to happen. When my time comes, you can bury me in an OP, but not before then. So what's it like in the SAS?'

'It's great.'

'You guys get to a lot of exciting places.'

Ricketts chuckled. 'Right. Like Belfast. So what do *you* think about the SAS? Does it bother you to have to work with us?'

'Not at all. In fact, I was thinking of applying when I get posted back to the mainland. I was in the Queen's Royal Lancers before being transferred to the Intelligence Corps, posted here for special duties, which meant 14 Intelligence Company. It's OK, but I need something with a little more variety. If your Lieutenant Cranfield's anything to go by, you guys must be all you're cracked up to be. Cranfield's like fucking James Bond! A real tough guy.'

A couple of Saracen armoured trucks, bristling with weapons and troops, passed the Q car, heading the other way, back to Bessbrook.

'A good officer,' Ricketts said. 'Being in Intelligence yourself, you probably appreciate the type.'

'We're not as free and easy in the Army as you are in the SAS. That's the difference between Captain Dubois and your Lieutenant Cranfield, as you probably noticed. Dubois's a good officer, but he tends to take his job pretty seriously. Cranfield, though good as well, is a lot more informal and headstrong. His SAS training, right?'

'More to do with his personality, I'd think,' Ricketts said, glancing at Gumboot and Martin in the mirror and receiving a wink from the first. 'Though he is, undoubtedly, quite a character and well known to be headstrong.'

From Gumboot's wink and Ricketts's tone, Martin sensed that Ricketts was leading to something specific.

'Absolutely,' Lovelock replied. 'Enough to have taken out that fucking IRA tout, no matter what he told you. Christ, Dubois' face was a picture. He *knows* it wasn't the IRA!'

'Is that the word about the place – that Cranfield did it?'

'Sure is. Him and Dubois and a couple of 14 Intelligence Company sergeants, they went out there and took him out. They did it for Phillips and the ten sources knocked off by the IRA. It was a pure revenge hit.'

'That isn't like the SAS,' Ricketts said.

'It's like Cranfield,' Lovelock insisted. 'Believe me, he did it – which is why Dubois was shitting himself when your friend raised the subject.'

'But Cranfield has never admitted he did it.'

'Of course not. He'd be in deep shit if he did. The killing has incensed the IRA and brought a lot of flak down on 14 Intelligence Company in general and the SAS in particular. That's why Dubois and Cranfield can't admit that they did it.'

'So what makes a lot of people think they did it?'

'Because Cranfield and Dubois have often sneaked across the border to snatch members of the IRA and bring them back to be captured, as it were, by the RUC. It's illegal, but they do it. Combine that knowledge with the fact that Cranfield was openly stating that he was going to avenge the suicide of Phillips, as well as the death of his ten sources and ... Well, what would *you* think?'

'I'd keep my thoughts to myself,' Ricketts replied.

'OK, Sarge, point taken.'

As they neared Belfast, a stretch of mountain loomed up out of the mist. Ricketts checked his

OS map, looked back up at the mountain and said, 'Divis, known locally as the Black Mountain.' Lovelock nodded his agreement as he left the motorway and entered Westlink.

'So this is the guided tour,' he said. 'We're now heading for the Grosvenor Road roundabout. When we get there, we'll drive along Grosvenor Road, past the Royal Victoria Hospital – where most of the kneecapped or otherwise wounded get treated – then head up the Springfield Road towards Turf Lodge, the heart of "Provo Land" – if it has a heart, that is.'

'It's that bad?'

'Fucking right. This is the worst killing ground in Europe and don't ever forget it.'

'What are the rules regarding the killings?'

'There aren't any. Though oddly enough, the Provos are more controlled than the Prods. The IRA are pretty methodical about who they kill or torture, whereas the loyalists tend to work on impulse – usually when they're angry. When they go for it, any victim will do – an innocent shopper, a teenager idling on a street corner, a pensioner in the bookie's – anyone convenient enough to be snatched. As for IRA tortures, they can't be any worse than what loyalists do with baseball bats, butcher's knives, or blowtorches. We find the victims hanging from fucking rafters and they're never a pretty sight. Freedom fighters? Don't even mention that word to me. These bastards are terrorists and psychopaths and should all be put down.'

Lovelock stopped the car at the Grosvenor Road roundabout, which was already busy. Eventually, when he had a clear run, he slipped into the traffic and turned into Grosvenor Road itself. Almost immediately, they passed a police station and regular Army checkpoint, surrounded by high, sandbagged walls and manned by heavily armed soldiers, all wearing DPM (Disruptive Pattern Material) clothing, helmets with chin straps and standard-issue boots. Apart from the private manning the 7.62mm L4 Light Machine Gun, the soldiers were carrying M16 rifles and had stun and smoke grenades on their webbing. The Q car was allowed to pass without being stopped. Further on, a soldier with an SA-80 assault rifle was keeping a Sapper covered while the latter carefully checked the contents of a rubbish bin. 'The Provos have Russian-manufactured RPG 7s,' Lovelock explained, 'which fire rocket-propelled grenades up to about 500 metres. The Provos use them mainly against police stations, army barracks and armoured "pigs" – they're troop carriers – and Saracen armoured cars. They also command-detonate dustbins filled with explosives from across the waste ground, which is why that Sapper's checking all the bins near the police station and the checkpoint. Usually, when explosives are placed in dustbins, it's done during the night, so the Sappers check this area every morning.'

Glancing out of his window, Martin saw that they were passing an enormous Victorian building on the left. When they reached the entrance, which was guarded by RUC officers wearing flak jackets and carrying the ubiquitous 5.56mm Ruger Mini-14 assault rifle, he saw ambulances inside and realized that it was the Royal Victoria Hospital.

'There it is,' Lovelock said sardonically. 'Kneecap Heaven. Go in there and you'll find them sitting or lying on stretchers, just waiting their turn. It's a daily occurrence – just part of the way of life here. It's fucking amazing what those bastards do to their own kind.'

'I thought they only did it to touts and other kinds of traitors,' Martin said, his curiosity aroused.

'No,' Lovelock said. 'They do it for a lot of things. Not wanting cops on their turf, the paramilitaries keep their own law, which means punishing car thieves, burglars, sex offenders, or so-called traitors in their own, rough fashion. Fuck, man, the people in these ghettos are so terrified of the IRA that when they receive a visit from them, saying they have to report for punishment, they actually go to the place selected for punishment of their own accord. Knowing what's going to happen to them, they sometimes try to anaesthetize themselves beforehand by getting pissed or bombed out on Valium. I mean, the whole business has become so routine, so *commonplace*, that the victims are even allowed to remove their pants or other clothing so they won't be damaged by the bullets. When the punishment's over, the paramilitaries will even call for an ambulance to take you away. You end up in that hospital, and often get compensation from the British government. If you do, you receive another visit from the guys who kneecapped you, demanding part of your compensation. Naturally, you hand it over with a big smile, before wobbling back to your bed of pain and nursing your wounds.'

This part of Belfast looked like London after the Blitz: rows of terraced houses with their doors and windows bricked up and gardens piled high with rubble. The pavements outside the pubs and certain shops were barricaded with large concrete blocks and sandbags. The windows were caged in heavy-duty wire netting as protection against car bombs and petrol bombers.

'OK,' Lovelock said. 'A few words of warning before we get into bandit country. Everything that Captain Dubois told you yesterday was true, but here's some more to remember. You can't leave a car in the streets. If you do, either it'll be vandalized by the kids; stolen for joyriding or to be sold or otherwise used by one of the paramilitary groups; or blown up by the Army because it might contain a bomb. Even if you leave it in a secure location, when returning to it you approach it from behind and bounce it on its springs, so as to trigger the small bomb that might have been planted under the driver's seat. Plan all journeys carefully before you leave and avoid enemy territory wherever possible. When driving, keep your windows locked at all times. If you're parked at a red light and someone approaches you, go through the red light and keep going until out of sight. If someone approaches you before you can move off, the only thing to say is: 'Fuck off!' If they don't, take off as quickly as possible. If you're in paramilitary territory and you knock someone down, don't stop. If you do, you'll be killed.'

The Grosvenor Road led across the Falls to Springfield, Ballymurphy and Turf Lodge, where everyone looked poor and suspicious, notably the gangs of young men – the 'dickers' – who stood menacingly on street corners, keeping their eyes out for newcomers or anything else they felt was threatening, particularly the SF patrols. Invariably, with the gangs, there were young people on crutches or with arms in slings, looking proud to be wounded.

'Have they been kneecapped?' Gumboot asked.

'Correct,' Lovelock replied. 'Look, you can even tell what kind of Catholic you're dealing with by checking just how he's been kneecapped. If it's a wound from a dainty little .22, which doesn't shatter bone, and it's either in a fleshy bit of the thigh or in the ankle, then the victim is only a minor thief or police informer. For something more serious he'll be shot in the back of the knee with a high-velocity rifle or pistol, which means the artery is severed and the kneecap blown right off. Now the six-pack, that's the major one, which makes you a real bad lot. With the six-pack he gets a bullet in each elbow, knee and ankle. That puts him on crutches for a long time and lets everyone see that he's a bad 'un. Now if that's what they can do to their own, what the hell do you think they're capable of when they drag an enemy, one of us, into an abandoned warehouse and string us up to the rafters for what they like to imagine is a bit of proper military interrogation?'

'I'd rather not dwell on it,' Martin said.

'Very wise,' Ricketts told him.

'Any quick way of telling the difference between Prods and Catholics?' Gumboot asked.

Lovelock laughed. 'Well, what can I say? A pigeon fancier is probably Protestant. A hurley player is definitely a Catholic, or Taig, as the Prods call them. Both sides play cricket, but only Orangemen are Rangers fans . . . and so on. You'll soon pick up the differences.'

He drove them around Turf Lodge to Andersonstown, then back to the Falls Road, the Provo heartland and one of the deadliest killing grounds in Northern Ireland – or anywhere else in the Western world. The streets of the 'war zone', as Lovelock called it, were clogged with armoured Land Rovers and forbidding army fortresses looming against the

70

sky. British Army barricades, topped with barbed wire and protected by machine-gun crews atop Saracen armoured cars, were blocking off the entrance to many streets, with the foot soldiers well armed and looking like Martians in their DPM uniforms, boots, webbing, camouflaged helmets and chin-protectors. The soldiers were checking everyone entering the barricaded areas and, in many instances, taking them aside to search them roughly.

'This is the heaviest security I've ever seen,' Ricketts said. 'To find it on British soil is just unbelievable.'

'And that's only the *visible* presence,' Lovelock replied. 'There are also static OPs with high-power cameras on the roofs of distant skyscrapers, recording every movement in these streets. There are also spies in the ceilings of suspected IRA buildings and bugs on the telephones. Caught between us and the IRA, ever vigilant in their more direct way, the people in these streets have little privacy, which only makes them more paranoid.'

Looking out and instinctively tightening his grip on his Browning, Martin noticed that the traffic was heading towards the distant Cave Hill. The black taxis were packed with passengers too frightened to use public transport or walk. Grey-painted RUC mobiles and British Army 'pigs' were passing constantly. In both kinds of vehicles, the officers were scanning the upper windows and roofs on either side of the road, looking for possible sniper positions.

'Look at 'em,' Lovelock said, indicating the men and youths loitering on street corners, the overweight housewives trudging wearily in and out of shops, and the grubby children who were clambering over a burnt-out car, smashing its remaining windows with sticks and screaming like banshees. 'Most of 'em don't give a fuck about a United Ireland; they simply give in to the paramilitaries out of fear. Believe me, if you had a nationwide election, Sinn Fein wouldn't stand a prayer of a chance against Fine Gael or Fianna Fáil. If that happened, the Prods would come under the rule of Dublin conservatives who hate the IRA as much as they do. Unfortunately, the dumb fucks don't see it that way. The political wing of the IRA is fighting a centuries-old war and the Prods are convinced that if the IRA wins, they, the loyalists, will be left to the mercy of the bloodthirsty Micks. It's all paranoid nonsense.'

Eventually, Lovelock ended up at the junction of the Falls Road and Springfield Road, back near the Royal Victoria Hospital, where he stopped the car and said: 'Hand me that camera.' When Ricketts passed him the Nikon, he wound the window down and took a lot of shots of the group of youths loitering across the road. Some had long hair, some had heads closely shaven, and all wore an assortment of casual, tatty jackets and had trousers rolled up high enough to reveal their big, unpolished boots. They looked sullen and dangerous.

Lovelock lowered the camera just before one of the youths looked directly at the car, then said something to his mates, all of whom stopped talking to each other and glanced across the road.

'They've seen us,' Lovelock said. 'That's because of this bloody car. The presence of a strange vehicle in these areas is generally noticed quickly – particularly as we mainly use relatively new British-made saloons, which I think is plain stupid. Outsiders, even innocent civilians, also become prey to republican gun law when kids like that, often armed, hijack cars for use by the IRA or INLA, or simply for the thrill of joyriding. Those little fuckers are dangerous.'

'Will they come over to check us out?' Ricketts asked.

'I don't think this particular bunch will. I think they know who we are. If they do, it means they're not a bunch of innocent kids. It means they're dickers – the ones who keep a lookout for the security forces and pass the word on to their superiors. They're probably in the IRA youth wing. No, they're not coming. They've decided to piss off.'

When the youths had moved away, making obscene gestures at the car and shouting insults that Martin, for one, couldn't quite make out, Lovelock wound the window up, then turned down

Grosvenor Road, back to the neutral territory of the city centre.

'Weird, isn't it?' he said, glancing out at the people streaming along the pavements, ignoring the armed soldiers carefully watching them. 'Most of those people out there are on the dole, supported by British money. This whole province is flooded with hand-outs from the British government. It actually pours more cash into here than it does into England. This fucking place is awash with British money. In fact, the whole place would sink if the British government withdrew its support. So these bastards are fighting the very people who keep them afloat. It doesn't make much sense, does it?'

By the time they arrived at the Protestant Shankill district, in the late afternoon, it had begun to rain. The sky was grey, the buildings were grimy, and the roads were lined with shabby shops and people wearing generally dark, unattractive clothing.

At the bottom of Grosvenor Road Lovelock turned into Sandy Row, a stoutly Protestant area, where he stopped the car again. It was a busy road, lined on both sides with shops and pubs, the pavements bustling with down-at-heel shoppers and the same kind of loiterers who had been so prevalent in the Catholic ghettos. Lovelock remained there for ten minutes, just holding his camera at the ready, then suddenly he wound down the window and took several shots of two men entering a pub across the road.

'A UDR watering-hole,' he explained, lowering the camera again. 'Full of hard-line loyalists. They do as much damage as the IRA, so we have to keep tabs on the bastards. I'm here today because this is collection day and those two are collecting protection money for a loyalist splinter group. This whole fucking city thrives on protection rackets, just like Al Capone ran. Anyone in business in the ghettos has to contribute, whether they like it or not. Falls Road cabbies make weekly payments to the IRA. Prods in Shankill pay similar levies to the UFF or UDA. Likewise with the owners of pubs, shops, betting shops, and people in the building trade. Most of the latter are now totally dependent on the work brought in by restoring or rebuilding bombed-out premises. Take away the Troubles, and you remove the livelihood of half of the populace. Truth of the matter is, the Troubles will never end because there's just too much fucking money in it. United Ireland? Freedom for the Irish people? That's all bullshit. It comes down to hard cash.'

When the two men emerged from the pub again, Lovelock took some more pictures, then put the camera down and jotted details in his notebook, including the time. When he had finished, he wound up the window and drove off.

'Fuck this for a lark,' he said. 'Let's go back to the Falls and see if we can get something worthwhile.'

They left Sandy Row, took the Donegal Road, then cut through the Broadway until they were back in the Falls Road. Lovelock parked well away from a dismal block of flats, by a waste ground filled with rubbish, where mangy dogs and scruffy, dirt-smeared children were playing noisily. He lowered the window, took the camera from Ricketts, and pointed to the high roof of the block of flats, which looked like a prison gone to seed. There, on the roof, was a British Army OP, its high-power telescope scanning the many people who loitered on the balconies or on the ground below, one soldier manning a General Purpose Machine Gun, or GPMG, others holding their M16 rifles, with the barrels resting lightly on the sandbagged wall.

'As you can see, they all know they're under surveillance,' Lovelock said.

'Do those overt OPs do any good?' Ricketts asked.

'Yes. They're equipped with computers linked to vehicle registration and suspect-information centres, as well as state-of-the-art surveillance cameras. Also, their high visibility reminds everyone of our presence and therefore places certain constraints on them, while allowing members of regular units and 14 Intelligence Company to observe suspects and see who their associates are. This in turn allows the collators of intelligence at Lisburn and brigade headquarters – including your so-called green slime – to investigate links between meetings of particular individuals and subsequent terrorist activities.'

'Do those OPs have any back-up?' Ricketts asked.

'Yes. Each OP is backed up by another OP consisting of two to four soldiers and located near enough to offer immediate firearms support. Both OPS are in turn backed up by a QRF, or Quick Reaction Force, of soldiers or police, sometimes both, located at the nearest convenient SF base, which will respond immediately to a radio call for help. So, no, they're not alone.'

'It's still fucking dangerous,' Gumboot said.

'Here everything is,' Lovelock replied. 'It's not a place to take lightly.'

Even as he spoke, the barrel of a Webley pistol was poked through the open window by his face and a harsh, youthful Ulster voice yelled: 'Get out of that fucking car!'

5

Everyone froze. 'Get out of that fucking car!' the youth screamed again, still aiming the pistol at Lovelock, but also tugging frantically at the locked door with his free hand. As he did so, another youth, just as scruffy in bomber jacket, jeans and big boots, with his head shaved close to the skull to make him look more brutal than perhaps he was, rushed out from behind a mound of rubble and tried to tug Gumboot's door open. Finding it locked, he kicked the car in frustration.

'Fuck off!' Lovelock said and made to start the car, but was stopped when the first youth reached in, grabbed his wrist with one hand and shoved the barrel of the Webley pistol into his face. 'One move and you're dead, you English cunt. Now get out of that fucking car.'

Lovelock removed his hands from the steering wheel and glanced across the waste ground to see another couple of youths running out of the flats, silhouetted in evening light, heading straight for the car. Before long, this few could grow into a crowd.

'OK, OK,' Lovelock said with a sigh. 'My hands are off the wheel. What's the matter with you, lad? We just came to visit some friends on the Falls and we lost our way.'

'Fucking army shite!' The youth tugged at the door again.

'We're not soldiers,' Lovelock lied. 'We're English, but not soldiers. We work in the building trade and we've come over to visit some old mates. We just got lost and pulled in here to check the map. For Christ's sake, be careful with that gun.'

'You lyin' bastard. The English don't have friends in Divis.' The kid tugged at the door again while his friend repeatedly kicked the rear door in a fury of frustration. 'Now open this fucking door or I'll blow your brains out.'

Seeing that another couple of youths were following the ones already racing towards them, Lovelock opened the door and stepped out of the car. The kid with the gun grabbed him by the shoulder and slammed him back against the car, then reached down for the camera, saying: 'Get that fucking back door open as well.'

Gumboot glanced at Martin, who was flushed with excitement, then unlocked his door and pushed it open. Martin did the same on his side and started getting out, though Ricketts remained where he was seated. Gumboot was still clambering out, about to stand upright, when the excited youth by his door punched him violently in the face.

Gumboot turned away from the blow, catching it on his cheek, almost falling back, but managing to stay standing. The other youth was about to grab the camera when he saw Ricketts sliding the OS map off his legs to reveal the Browning High Power on his lap.

'Fuck!' Jerking back to straighten up and fire at Ricketts, the kid banged the back of his head on the door frame and yelped with pain as his mate was taking another punch at Gumboot. The kid with the pistol threw himself away from the door as Ricketts swung up his Browning and Gumboot cross-drew his from its holster and aimed it two-handed at his assailant.

As Lovelock jumped back into the driver's seat, Ricketts rolled backwards out of his side, the kid with the pistol aimed at the car, and the other started running away from Gumboot. Lovelock turned the ignition key and gunned the engine. Ricketts fired a burst single-handed at the kid with the Webley. The burst picked the kid up and flung him on his back even as Martin, feeling extraordinarily bright, steadied his wrists on the roof of the Q car and fired a burst two-handed over the heads of the youths racing to help their mates.

Gumboot let his assailant go, aware that he was unarmed, then he turned towards the youths whom Martin had fired at. Some were scattering, others flinging themselves to the ground. Gumboot fired over their heads to ram Ricketts's message home, then he and Ricketts dived simultaneously back into the car.

Martin just about managed to get back into his seat when Lovelock reversed at high speed, bouncing backwards up over the pavement and smashing into a wall, before doing a sharp, screeching U-turn and racing away from the flats.

'Shit!' he exclaimed.

Looking through the rear window, Martin saw the youths picking themselves up from the rubble and racing towards the one who had been shot by Ricketts. He was lying spread-eagled, not moving, his chest covered in blood.

'I didn't have a choice,' Ricketts said. 'He was aiming right at me.'

'Those fucking kids weren't amateurs,' Lovelock said. 'To see us that quickly the little pricks had to be on the look out. They were dickers.'

Still glancing back, Martin saw some of the youths hurling stones in frustration, knowing that they couldn't possibly hit the car, but feeling impelled to do something. Meanwhile, the others were gathering around the youth shot, and almost certainly killed, by Ricketts.

'Jesus!' Martin whispered.

'He won't help,' Gumboot informed him. 'The only thing that's gonna help us is to get the fuck out of here.'

Ricketts twisted in his seat to glance back over his shoulder as Lovelock took a corner, practically on two wheels. 'You were very good, Martin,' he said. 'You didn't put a foot wrong. You deliberately fired above their heads, didn't you?'

'Yes,' Martin said.

'You've just earned your badge.' Ricketts turned back to the front as Lovelock slowed down, trying to look like a normal driver, and edged into the Falls Road.

Looking out at the bricked-up doorways, boarded shop windows, wired, sandbagged pubs, weary pedestrians, heavily armed soldiers, flak-jacketed RUC officers, barricaded streets and gangs of watchful youths or screaming, destructive children, Martin thought of what Ricketts had said to him and swelled up with pride.

You've just earned your badge, he thought to himself.

'Fuck it,' Lovelock said. 'Those kids were on the look out. That means they were in the IRA youth wing and that means we have to know who they are. Did anyone get a good look at them?'

'I got a good look at the fucker who punched me in the face,' Gumboot said, instinctively rubbing his swollen cheekbone with his fingers. 'If I hadn't turned my head, he'd have taken out my teeth, so I'm certainly gonna remember the little shit. I *want* to remember him!'

'And the others?'

'They were close enough for me to recognize a few,' Ricketts said, amazing Martin with how steady he sounded so soon after having killed a man. 'If I saw them again, I could pick them out.'

'A line-up?'

'Sounds good,' Ricketts said.

'Right.' Lovelock, while driving with one hand, removed the Landmaster III transceiver from its webbed harness and contacted the local commander of the Springfield Road Barracks. When the commander identified himself with a broad Ulster accent, Lovelock told him about the incident and requested a sweep of the area to locate and bring in as many youths as possible for a line-up.

'Did you say one dead?' the commander responded.

'Yes,' Lovelock said. 'He was about to fire at us with a Webley pistol, so all options were closed.'

'That could cause a lot of trouble.'

'I repeat: there was no option. The youth was about to fire a round and there was no time for talk.'

'A youth?'

'Yes.'

'Not an adult.'

'No.'

'Are you certain he was dead?'

'Yes,' Ricketts said.

'Then we're in for some trouble.'

'Sorry,' Lovelock said, 'but we still need that sweep.'

'Be at Castlereagh at precisely eight this evening. Until then, stay low.'

'Right,' Lovelock said. 'Over and out.' He switched off the Landmaster III, returned it to its webbing, and checked his wristwatch while still driving along the Falls Road. 'That leaves us with two hours to kill,' he said, 'so what do we do?' When no one replied, he said: 'I have to have a talk with one of my touts, so let's head back to the centre of town. While I'm having my chat, you men can stay in the car and have your sandwiches and coffee. When I'm done, we'll come back here and see how the sweep's progressing, then go on to Castlereagh.'

'Are you fucking crazy?' Gumboot said. 'I mean, coming back here!'

'We'll be OK,' Lovelock said. 'By the time we get back here the sweep will be well under way and the fuckers on that estate will be too busy to take any notice of us. What do you say, Sarge?'

'I agree.'

Lovelock drove them to the centre of Belfast, then on to a pub opposite the Europa Hotel, which, having been bombed a few times, was now guarded like a military camp.

After parking, Lovelock nodded in the direction of the pub. 'It's a neutral pub that gets the fall-out from Sandy Row. I meet my loyalist tout in there. You can come with me, Ricketts.'

When he got out of the car, Ricketts did the same. Lovelock then opened the back door and indicated that Gumboot should get out too. When

Gumboot had done so, Lovelock said: 'Take the driver's seat. You get up front, as well, Martin. Just sit there, enjoying the view, having your hot tea and sandwiches. If you get checked by any army or RUC patrols – which almost certainly you will – show your ID. When they see it, they'll know you're in a Q car and leave you alone. On the other hand, if you're approached by anyone else – a civilian – be prepared for trouble. If you have to take off, give a long toot on your horn, so Ricketts and I will know you're going. If you take off, don't return for us; just go on to Castlereagh. Any questions?'

'Yeah,' Gumboot said, picking his wrapped sandwiches and vacuum flask off the back seat, slamming the door, then sliding into the driver's seat. 'What's in the sandwiches?'

'Mick turd with mayonnaise,' Lovelock said as Martin got out of the back, also holding a pack of sandwiches, and slipped into the seat beside Gumboot. 'Don't forget to keep the doors locked and the windows wound up. If you see anything of interest, the camera's in the glove compartment. The transceiver's on the floor between you. Enjoy your meal, men.'

'Don't drink on duty,' Martin said with a grin.

'Wouldn't dream of it,' Ricketts replied. 'But if I have to have one in the line of duty, I'll be thinking of you.'

'Fuck off,' Gumboot said.

Ricketts automatically checked that his Browning was well concealed beneath his jacket as he followed Lovelock into the pub. It was an expansive Victorian place with lots of tiles, mahogany and stained-glass windows. It had a long bar and plenty of tables spaced well apart. There were few people at the tables and only one man was sitting on a bar stool – at the end near the entrance.

Leading Ricketts up to the middle of the bar, Lovelock loudly asked him what he'd like to drink. The authenticity of his Ulster accent took Ricketts by surprise, but he managed to hide it and ordered a pint of Guinness in low tones. Lovelock ordered the same for himself, still speaking loudly and like an Ulsterman. He glanced at the lone man near the entrance, then paid the barman, handed Ricketts his Guinness, and led him to a table in the far corner of the pub, where a middle-aged man in oily overalls was savouring a whisky while reading the *Belfast Telegraph*.

'It's no use pretending to read, Norman, I know damned well you can't.'

The man looked up, glanced at his wristwatch, then said without a trace of irony: 'Have you arrived?'

'I have.' Lovelock took the chair beside the man, which meant he could keep his eyes on the entrance. He nodded for Ricketts to take the seat at the other side of him, which placed him in view of the toilets and, possibly, the back door. 'This is an English friend, Phil Ricketts. We used to work together in London, before I saw sense and came home. Phil, this is Norman Reid.'

Ricketts nodded.

'Nice to meet ya, Phil. First time in Belfast?'

'Yes,' Ricketts said.

'A queer wee place, right?'

'It takes some getting used to.'

'What's that you're drinking?' Lovelock asked, still using his Ulster accent, but more softly now.

'Bushmills.'

'A dangerous brew.'

'Ach, well, sure it warms the stomach on a winter's evening.' He had another sip, then glanced at the man sitting at the bar near the entrance. 'Now mind what yer sayin'. That one at the end of the bar is from Sandy Row. Be natural, but keep yer voice low, and he won't hear from here.'

'UDA?'

Reid nodded. 'He's an ijit, but he lives for the cause and is here for the money.'

'Protection?'

'Aye. But he's also here to check out who comes in and he can be right nasty. A dunderhead, but dangerous.'

'Anything to tell me?'

'You heard about the shootin' up near Divis?'

'News travels fast.'

'It does in this wee city. They say the Mick was shot by men in plain clothes and now the

Army are sweeping the area for the other lads involved.'

'The men in plain clothes weren't identified?'

'Na. But no doubt you have yer own ideas.'

'Not so far,' Lovelock said.

'So how'd ya hear about it so quickly, like?'

'We heard it over our car radio. So what's happening down Sandy Row way?'

'They're tickled pink over the fact that another Mick has been killed by the Army.'

'Unidentified,' Lovelock reminded him.

'Aye, unidentified – like an Army Q car's unidentified. They all know it was Army. They think it'll lead to Provisional IRA retaliation, which will give them an excuse for another bloodbath. They're all sittin' down there oilin' their guns with big grins on their mugs. It's as good as the killin' of O'Halloran, they say, so you can expect a wee comeback for that.'

'What kind of comeback?'

'Comeback in kind. I'd say the Micks will go for Lieutenant Cranfield, so he'd best watch his wee English arse. He's done youse all some damage, like.'

Reid talked for another twenty or minutes or so, giving Lovelock an update on what was happening in the pubs of Sandy Row between the members of the UDA and other Protestant paramilitary groups. He passed no written information to Lovelock, but dropped a few names for him to place watches on, with details of where they were most likely to be found. When he had finished, Lovelock thanked him, finished his beer, then left the pub with Ricketts, walking past the UDA man sitting at the bar and keeping his eye on the door. The man studied them carefully as they left, but was distracted when another customer entered, allowing Lovelock and Ricketts to leave without questioning.

The Q car was still parked outside, with Gumboot and Martin, having finished their sandwiches and tea, studying the busy road in a bored manner. Darkness had fallen and the street lights were on, as were the headlights of the many cars and buses of the rush-hour traffic. Across the road, the lights of the Europa Hotel burned brightly, beaming down over the fenced-in courtyard and the huts of the private security guards.

Lovelock knocked on the side window of the car with his knuckles, then jerked his thumb towards the rear. 'OK,' he said, 'out!' Gumboot opened the door, clambered out and got in the back as Lovelock took his place in the driver's seat. Martin did likewise, allowing Ricketts to sit beside Lovelock. 'Any problems?' Lovelock asked, turning on the ignition.

'No problems,' Gumboot said, 'but we were questioned by RUC and Army patrols every ten or fifteen minutes. In fact, every patrol that passed stopped to question us.'

'They would. You can't sit in a parked car in Belfast without being questioned. They were OK when you showed them your ID?'

'Yeah, no bother. They just tipped their peaked caps and moved on. All very polite, like.'

'You're beginning to sound Irish already, like.'

Gumboot grinned. 'It's contagious, like.'

Glancing constantly back over his shoulder, Lovelock edged into the dense traffic, cut through to Bedford Street, then drove down Dublin Road. At Shaftesbury Square he turned into Donegal Road and drove from there, through Broadway, to the Falls Road, which, in the darkness, illuminated by the street lights, looked even more dangerous than it had during the day.

The gangs of men, young and old, standing on street corners seemed larger, with many drinking from cans or bottles and clearly aggressive. The bricked-up doorways and boarded-up windows were only rendered more ominous by the light-streaked darkness. Children smashing parked cars without reprimand from frightened passers-by seemed like scavenging animals. The RUC officers in their flak jackets and the heavily armed soldiers at the sandbagged barracks and barricaded streets, all watchful, never smiling, seemed like faceless men in a bad dream.

Even before the tower block came into view, the crimson glow of flames was illuminating the dark, cloudy sky and the sound of sporadic gunfire could be heard. When Lovelock finally turned off the Falls Road and reached the spot where they had almost been hijacked, they saw mobiles and foot patrols trawling the flats, which were being swept eerily by spotlights. The red glow in the sky came from a series of bonfires deliberately started to block the paths of the mobiles and Saracens, as well as frustrate the charges of the soldiers in flak jackets, perspex-visored riot helmets and reinforced leg and arm shields.

Other fires were caused by the Molotov cocktails being thrown by gangs of teenage dickers. People were screaming when struck by rubber bullets. Others were racing out of clouds of CS gas with eyes streaming. Housewives were drumming bin lids on the concrete floors and balconies, children and youths were throwing stones and dropping bricks on the mobiles thwarted by the bonfires, and unseen men were sniping on the soldiers keeping watch while their mates smashed in doors with sledgehammers and dragged out kicking, punching youths for transportation to the detention block at Castlereagh.

'It's a fucking nightmare,' Gumboot said in the back of the parked car as they watched the distant soldiers drag struggling youths from the walkways of the tower block to the waiting RUC vans. By now, however, the youths' ankles were chained together to prevent them from kicking out or running away.

'This is just another night in Belfast,' Lovelock corrected him sardonically. 'See that,' he added, pointing to where the youths were being practically dragged to the waiting vans. 'The housewives here talk about how they've been handcuffed by the feet. It's a wonderful language.'

'We'd better get to Castlereagh,' Ricketts said.

'I think you're right, Sarge.'

Lovelock turned the car around and drove away from the hellish scene, out of the Falls, back through the city centre, across the Albert Bridge, then along the A23 to Castlereagh.

Arriving at the detention barracks just before 8 p.m., they were directed to the rear of the building by an armed, uniformed RUC guard. Lovelock parked the car in what looked like an enormous yard, like an empty car park, with a high brick wall running along one end. He turned the ignition off, then the headlights, leaving them in almost total darkness.

'Now we wait,' he said, checking his watch. 'It should start any minute now.'

Suddenly, a series of arc lights flared into life along the top of the wall the car was facing, bathing the wall and the ground in front in a dazzling white light. Less than a minute later, a couple of armed RUC officers emerged from a door at one end of the wall to take up positions at both ends of the wall, about twenty feet away, covering it with their 5.56mm Ruger Mini-14 assault rifles. When they were in position, first one, then two, then a whole group of dishevelled youths were coaxed out through the door and along the base of the wall by another RUC officer. When some of the youths, either blinded by the light or frightened, took a step back, the RUC officer prodded them forward with his baton. If this failed, he gave them a light blow with it, and this always worked. Eventually the youths, nearly a dozen, were standing along the whole length of the wall, an equal distance apart, figures in an eerily dreamlike chiaroscuro.

'Well?' Lovelock asked. 'Who do we recognize?'

'That little bastard who punched me,' Gumboot said. 'Fifth from the left.'

'Good,' Lovelock said. 'Anyone else?'

'Yes,' Ricketts said. 'I recognize two of the bunch we fired at.'

'Any more?'

'No.'

'Right,' Lovelock said. 'When they step forward, tap me on the shoulder and I'll toot my horn.'

At a barked command from the RUC officer with the baton, the youth who had been first out of the doorway and was now standing at the far left of the line, stepped forward, where he could be seen more clearly. The RUC officer glanced at the car parked in darkness, outside the range of the arc lights. He heard no toot, and ordered the first youth back against the wall, before calling out the second youth. When there was still no response, he ordered the third youth to step forward. When Lovelock tooted his horn, the youth was dragged out of the line-up and led through the doorway by another armed guard. This process continued until Lovelock tooted his horn again and another youth was pulled out of the line-up and taken away. When the third youth was identified and led away, the parade continued until the last youth had stepped forward and been ordered back. Then the remaining members of the line-up were marched back through the doorway for release and return to Belfast.

When the last of the RUC officers had followed the young men through the door, the arc lights blinked out, plunging the wall back into pitch darkness.

'I think we've all earned a beer,' Lovelock said. 'Your first day is finished, lads.'

He turned the car around and drove them back through the dark, stormy night to the camp at Bessbrook.

6

Wearing civilian clothing, but with two different sets of ID papers – one genuine, the other false ones for a fictitious Ulster resident – and with his Browning holstered in the cross-draw position under his coat, Lieutenant Cranfield drove halfway along the Falls Road in a car with Belfast number plates. He parked near the Broadway, checked his watch and waited patiently for his tout to arrive.

The Falls was a lot quieter than it had been yesterday when, after the shooting, the commander of the Springfield Road Barracks had instigated a cordon-and-search sweep of the area, thus sparking off another riot on the block of flats on the Divis estate, with the usual bonfires, hurled stones and drumming bin lids. As the dead youth was only sixteen years old, the republican papers had been filled with the usual sanctimonious outrage, including demands for the boy's 'murderer' to be brought to justice. That so-called 'murderer', as Cranfield knew, was the excellent Sergeant Phil Ricketts.

Well, Cranfield thought with a grin, *young Martin Renshaw certainly had an interesting first day in Belfast.*

As was customary, when the various Q-car teams had returned to the camp, they had first signed in their weapons, then reported to Captain Dubois and Lieutenant Cranfield in the briefing room. The meeting with Lovelock, Ricketts, Gumboot and young Renshaw had been more tense than most, particularly when Ricketts confessed that he was the unidentified man who had shot and killed the youth on the Divis estate.

Luckily, by the time of that meeting, Dubois had already received identification of the victim, passed it on to Intelligence, and learnt from them that he was an active member of the IRA youth wing. Naturally, this fact would be denied by the IRA, who would want to use the kid's 'murder' for all the propaganda value they could wring from it. Ricketts, a smart man, had been concerned about that possibility, but Cranfield had put him at his ease, accepting that he'd had no choice in the matter and noting in his report that Sergeant Lovelock and the others present had confirmed that this was indeed the case.

Now, gazing across the Falls Road to see the usual sorry mixture of armed soldiers, sullen or taunting youths, screeching children, and wearily shopping housewives, all rendered more depressing in the grey afternoon light, Cranfield, though vigilant and wary, was at ease with himself. His men, he felt, had behaved impeccably in a bad situation. Contrary to the concern expressed by the overly concerned Captain Dubois, the SAS men had done what was necessary.

Five minutes later, dead on time, Cranfield's tout, Michael O'Leary, slipped into the car and said tersely: 'OK, take off.' Cranfield pulled out into the traffic and headed along the Falls Road, away from the Broadway. 'No camera,' O'Leary said. 'No notebook. Drive slowly, but steadily. Don't slow down when I point anything out. Understood?'

'Yes,' Cranfield said.

It annoyed him that O'Leary should give him this redundant advice when they'd done this so many times. On the other hand, the Irishman was probably more nervous than usual.

Still a member of the provisional IRA, O'Leary had been the bookkeeper for his local wing and started fiddling the books when he became involved with an exceptionally attractive, financially demanding lady named Margaret Dogherty. O'Leary was a sexually inexperienced bachelor who couldn't believe his luck when he met Margaret in his favourite Republican club and ended up in her bed. Margaret was not only beautiful, but superb in bed. O'Leary was soon head-over-heels in love and half out of his mind with desire.

Margaret, however, liked the good life and O'Leary had to pay for it, which led to his 'borrowing' from the funds of his local PIRA branch. When he found he couldn't replace the money, he 'borrowed' more and tried to recoup his loss at the bookie's. When this didn't work, he kept borrowing until he was in so deep, he was desperate. Finally, when it was time for an audit of the books and he knew his thefts would be revealed to his PIRA superiors, he tearfully confided in Margaret, who introduced him to a man who could help him.

This man turned out to be a member of British Intelligence, MI5, who had put Margaret on to O'Leary in the first place. MI5 agreed to repay O'Leary before the audit and also finance him on a regular basis in the future on the grounds that he 'turn' and become their tout. Terrified of being punished by PIRA – which for his offence could have been terminal after torture – and also still besotted with Margaret, who was in fact a high-class prostitute operating out of Dublin, O'Leary agreed.

Nevertheless, he was still a troubled man, knowing that the longer he touted, the greater were his chances of being discovered. When the affair with Margaret abruptly ended – having done her job, she returned to Dublin – O'Leary, no longer blinded by love, had become even more frightened. As he had told Cranfield over the phone, he wanted to be 'lifted out' and given a new identity, in return for which he would give Cranfield a 'big one'. He was going to do so today, which is why he was nervous.

'Has it been arranged?' he asked as they drove up the Falls Road.

'It's been agreed,' Cranfield replied. 'We just need to know your final destination and when you want it to be.'

'Australia.'

'Whereabouts?'

'Anywhere.'

'When?'

'Two weeks, like.'

'Why wait that long?'

'I have to have a yarn with someone in Dublin.'

Cranfield smiled. *How wondrous is love*, he thought. 'That could be leaving it too long,' he said, 'if you're as concerned as you sounded on the phone. *Are* you that concerned?'

'Yeah.'

'Why?'

'I think they suspect me. I've been seen in too many places with m'girlfriend, spending the kind of loot I shouldn't have. Sooner or later, they'll want t'know where I got it.'

'If that's true, you better leave next week.'

'I have to have m'wee yarn first.'

Cranfield shrugged. 'As you wish. Two weeks from today?'

'Aye,' O'Leary said, scanning the busy pavements on both sides of the road. 'That'll do a treat.'

They were silent for a moment, then Cranfield asked: 'So, what's the big one?'

'You,' O'Leary replied without the slightest trace of irony. 'They believe you're the one who copped O'Halloran and they're goin' t'get ya.'

'What makes them think I did it?'

'Ach, come on, man! They know you and Dubois have often crossed the border to snatch men and bring 'em back t'the RUC. Knowing that, they figured it had t'be you who did O'Halloran in. If it *wasn't* you, it doesn't matter a damn. They want a high profile and you've got it; so it's you they'll be gunnin' for. It's also retaliation fer that lad shot dead yesterday.'

'Do they have a suspect for that?'

'Na,' O'Leary said. 'They just talk about the British bastard and say he was one of yours – SAS, like.'

The car had stopped at traffic lights and Cranfield glanced out at a group of men and youths loitering threateningly on the street corner, outside a betting shop that had windows caged in heavy-duty wire netting. When Cranfield noticed that one of the men was on crutches, he felt distinctly uneasy and was glad when the car moved on through the lights. 'So what are you offering?'

'The gits chosen t'hit ya.'

'All of them?'

'Aye. It's a PIRA Active Service Unit of four men. Part of the wing I keep the books for. They're the ones that took out your ten sources before Phillips killed himself. You've been wanting them anyway.'

'Damn, yes!' Cranfield whispered.

'The leader, Michael Quinn, lives right opposite me. He and the others meet reg'larly in his house. When they're not there, they're usually in the streets spyin' an' accusin', holdin' summary trials in back rooms, or personally supervisin' the punishments. I'll point them out to ya. Ya can't take pictures or be seen jottin' notes, so remember their mugs as best ya can.'

'I want more than that.'

'Yer goin' t'get it. Just bide yer time.'

When they stopped at the next traffic lights, O'Leary said: 'Have a look at that bunch on the corner without makin' it obvious. D'ya see them?'

Cranfield turned his head left while ostensibly scratching his right cheek. He saw a bunch of men on the street corner. Four were in their teens, all with short-cropped hair, dressed in the usual scruffy bomber jackets, jeans and big boots, and drinking from cans of extra-strong beer. They were listening intently, nervously, to a man in a soiled gaberdine raincoat. Grey-haired and with a hard, angry face, he was jabbing his forefinger at them as he spoke.

'Yes,' Cranfield said, 'I see them.'

'Four kids and an older man, right?'

'Right.'

'Ignore the kids – they're just dickers. The older

man is Michael Quinn. He's the leader of the PIRA unit chosen to take you out – the one who lives opposite me.' The traffic lights changed to green and they drove on, sticking to a relatively slow, steady pace. 'We'll soon be reaching another book-ie's,' O'Leary said. 'A few hundred yards up on the left. Don't slow down – just scan 'im as quickly as possible. He's called Patrick Mulgrew. He collects the protection money from that bookie's and he's there to check people comin' in an' out. He's part of the hit team.'

Even before the car reached the betting shop, Cranfield saw the man standing outside, hunched against the wind in his gaberdine raincoat and blowing into his frozen hands. As they passed him, Cranfield studied his profile, then his full face – hollow-cheeked, thin-lipped, dark circles under the eyes.

'I've got him,' he said.

'Right,' O'Leary replied. 'I live in the next street. Everyone enterin' or leavin' is checked by PIRA members workin' on shifts in four-man teams – two men at each end of the street. Today the men at this end are the other two picked t'hit you. Try t'check them as we turn into the street. Drive slowly and don't stare. If ya haven't enough time, turn around and come back out again.'

'OK,' Cranfield said.

As the car reached the corner, Cranfield saw the two men standing at the far side of the street, both smoking and watching those coming and going. 'That's them,' O'Leary confirmed. Cranfield managed to scan their faces and remember the details before the car straightened out and headed along the street.

'OK,' he said. 'Got them.'

'The one on the right – nearest the Falls – was Seamus McGrath. The one on the left, nearest to us, was John Houlihan. Like Quinn, they're hard men. Very experienced. That's why they've been picked.' They drove along the street, past rows of two-up, two-down terraced houses. 'We'll soon be reachin' number thirty-seven,' O'Leary said. 'That's the home of Michael Quinn, the leader of the pack. He lives there with 'is missus – his kids are all married – but he sends her t'the bingo when his mates come around. As I said, they meet regular, like – two or three times a week. The house directly opposite, number thirty-eight, is mine.' Cranfield glanced at both houses as he drove past. 'As you know,' O'Leary said when they had passed, 'I live there alone. So you get the Army to do a sweep of the street as cover while you move some men into m'loft for yer covert OP. While the sweep's on, ya can bug Quinn's house and hide anything else yer goin' t'need. Ya keep tabs on that lot and then move against 'em at yer leisure. Ya have to set it up before I leave. Take 'em out when I'm gone.'

'I will,' Cranfield said.

*   *   *

Cranfield dropped O'Leary off where he had picked him up, near the Broadway, then drove back to the centre of town to the Europa Hotel. After being thoroughly checked by the private security guards, he was allowed to drive through the electronically controlled gates and park in the part of the forecourt enclosed by heavy-duty wire fencing and used as a car park.

He went straight to the first-floor lounge bar, where he purchased a Bushmills at the counter. As usual, the bar was busy, mostly with journalists from London, male and female, most of whom smoked like trains, drank like fish, and talked in loud voices on the bar stools or in soft chairs and sofas placed around tables spaced well apart.

Not wishing to be engaged in conversation, but always keen to listen, Cranfield sat at the bar until an empty table became available. Shortly afterwards, Captain Dubois entered, wearing an immaculate pinstripe suit, a shirt and tie, and highly polished black shoes. Having ordered a whisky at the bar, he sat down facing Cranfield. He did not look too happy.

'Why do you always insist on meeting here?' he asked. 'This place is swarming with reporters from London.'

'I'm starved for attractive women,' Cranfield replied, 'and Fleet Street has lots of them.'

Dubois glanced automatically around the packed,

smoky bar, taking note of a couple of very appealing ladies, then he turned back to Cranfield.

'Keep your mind on your work,' he said. 'So, what's the business?'

'We kicked up a bit of a dust storm,' Cranfield said, 'and the debris is raining down.'

Dubois glanced right and left, as if nervous about being overhead, then looked directly at Cranfield again. 'O'Halloran?' Cranfield nodded assent. 'So what's the dust storm?' When Cranfield related what he had just learnt from O'Leary, Dubois looked even less pleased. 'Christ,' he said. 'As if it wasn't bad enough with all this flak in the papers about SAS assassinations. I'm beginning to think, Cranfield, that you're causing me more trouble than you're worth.'

'The SAS get blamed for a lot of things they've never done.'

'We all know who topped O'Halloran.'

'I should remind you that you were present.'

'As for that stone-thrower yesterday . . .'

'He was about to fire a Webley pistol.'

'Nevertheless, it was your damned SAS man who . . .'

'Don't forget,' Cranfield interjected, enjoying Dubois' discomfort, 'that it wasn't just the SAS involved. The driver, indeed the man in charge of the team, was your own Sergeant Lovelock.'

Dubois rolled his eyes and glanced across the

room, momentarily distracted from his own concerns by the long, shapely legs of a woman smoking and drinking at the bar. Perhaps remembering that she was almost certainly a journalist, Dubois shook his head again and sipped some whisky.

'Am I included in their hit list?' he asked.

'No.'

'I'm delighted to hear it. They want only you.'

'That appears to be the case.'

'You don't appear to be concerned.'

'I'm not. I'm planning to get them first.'

'How?'

'I know who they are. O'Leary pointed them out to me. He lives directly opposite the house they meet in, so I'm going to call for a cordon-and-search sweep of the street and plant an OP in O'Leary's place. The PIRA house will be bugged at the same time. We keep tabs on them and move when we're good and ready, knowing just where they'll be.'

Dubois thought about it. 'This is getting tricky,' he said. 'I've a feeling that we've stirred up too much with that single cross-border hit.'

'The ones we've stirred up are the bastards who took out our ten sources and caused Phillips's suicide. If we take them out, it'll look like retaliation, which is the kind of language their mates will understand. It'll give us the edge and begin the required cleansing of Belfast and, later, south Armagh.'

Startled, Dubois stared at Cranfield. 'Is that what you're after?'

'Yes,' Cranfield said.

'You're too ambitious for your own good, Lieutenant.'

'Don't ever mention rank in this bar.'

'I'm so sorry, Cranfield, but the accusation stands.'

Cranfield grinned. 'I don't believe in the concept of too much ambition. I believe in doing what's necessary. And whatever's necessary to clean up Northern Ireland, is what I'm willing to do.'

'You're going against the grain of your own Regiment,' Dubois said. 'The Regiment admires initiation, but not big timing – and that's what you're starting to do by taking matters, including the law, into your own hands. A certain independence of spirit has always been admired in the Regiment, but you're wildly overstepping the mark.'

'I don't know what you mean.'

'You shouldn't have crossed the border without permission, let alone put a stop to someone there.

'Then you shouldn't have helped me.'

'That's true.'

'Listen,' Cranfield said, leaning across the table to place his hand on Dubois' wrist and gaze intently at him. 'This bloody business in Northern Ireland has been going on too long, with the whole of the British intelligence and military complex being humiliated by a bunch of former amateurs. Sooner or later this has to be stopped, but it won't be as long as we abide by the rules while the IRA's completely disregarding them. There's no Geneva Convention here. There are no Queensberry rules. We've been sent over here to finally clean out the whole area, and if we have to do what they do to succeed, then damn it, let's do it.'

'Hence O'Halloran and that lad yesterday.'

'O'Halloran was planned, the lad yesterday wasn't, but the two combined have clearly succeeded in bringing those bastards out of the closet. Now that they're out, let's get them and put an end to it.'

'My God!' Dubois said. 'You really mean it. You think you can win this whole war.'

'I can certainly try,' Cranfield said. He sat back in his chair, glanced at the ladies on the bar stools, then returned his steady, hazel-eyed gaze to Dubois. 'Stop worrying about O'Halloran,' he said. 'What we did, did the trick.'

Dubois sipped some whisky, ran his forefinger around the glass, then shook his head again from side to side.

'Damn it,' he said bitterly. 'We shouldn't have done it. My first instincts were right. Now we've got a damned range war on our hands and the blame will lie squarely with the SAS.'

'Or 14 Intelligence Company,' Cranfield reminded him.

'Even worse,' Dubois said.

'You see it as wrong; I see it as right,' Cranfield said. 'Let's have a damned range war. Let them come out of the woodwork. We want to break the IRA in south Armagh and this opens that gate. They're showing their faces at last and we're going to take them out.'

'We'd better,' Dubois said.

7

'So what the fuck did *you* do?' Gumboot asked Jock McGregor over a beer in the busy NAAFI canteen in Bessbrook. He was sitting at a long table with Jock, Ricketts, Sergeant Lampton, Danny 'Baby Face' Porter, 'Taff' Burgess, the recently 'blooded' Martin, and the British Army sergeant, Ralph Lovelock.

As usual, Sergeant 'Dead-eye Dick' Parker was drinking all alone at the bar, not smiling at anyone.

'You mean apart from topping fucking teenagers and starting the Third World War?'

'That teenager had a Webley pistol and was ready to use it,' Martin, who was growing bolder, reminded Jock. 'So Ricketts had no choice.'

'You don't aim to wound,' Danny agreed, speaking as quietly, as shyly, as always. 'Lieutenant Cranfield confirmed that.'

'He would,' Sergeant Lampton said. 'Lieutenant Cranfield is a man who likes action and goes looking for it.'

'No bad thing,' Danny replied.

'It can be,' Lampton said. 'This isn't Oman, where the enemy was clear-cut. It's a war on British soil and we're subject to British laws, so certain actions have to be accounted for. If you shoot the wrong man here, you could find yourself on trial with a life sentence hanging over your head. So going to look for action here isn't a wise thing to do.'

'Right,' Ricketts said. 'I agree completely, Frank. I had to shoot that kid – he was getting ready to shoot me – but the local papers, as well as the IRA, are already talking about murderers and demanding justice. You wouldn't get that in Oman, nor in Malaya. So you don't go looking for trouble in this place, and, even if you happen to find it, you certainly have to look before you leap.'

'Correct,' Lampton said. 'In case you break the law, if nothing else. An awful lot of British soldiers have been put on trial just because they lost their cool and shot the wrong bloody person. That's why you don't seek it out.'

'So what did you do, Jock?' Gumboot repeated. 'Apart from jacking off to pass the time?'

'Apart from jacking off, the same as you,' Jock said. 'We just drove around – me, Danny, Dead-eye Dick, and a sergeant from 14 Intelligence Company.'

'Sergeant Hampton,' Lovelock informed them.

'Yeah, right,' Jock agreed. 'Sergeant Hampton.

Good bloke. We saw the sights, took pictures, wrote notes on what we'd seen, and in general got to know the city. What a fucking nightmare! Schoolkids wrecking cars, teenagers grilling you at traffic lights, fat hags spitting at the soldiers and police, all of them acting like they were barefoot on razors. Buildings burnt out, bombed out, boarded up, with their windows, if not smashed, covered in heavy-duty mesh wire. Tanks and armoured pigs. Sniper fire at least once every hour. A maze of backstreets and narrow, dark alleys, perfect for killing. A right piss-hole, in fact.'

'Where on earth did *you* go?' Taff asked.

'Andersonstown, Mountpottinger, the Falls, Whiterock, the Ardoyne, that bloody Ballymurphy Bull Ring – when not wanking, of course. We've seen it all, Taff, and we're really looking forward to our stay here.'

'At least we don't have to deal with flying beetles, hornets, red and black ants, centipedes, camel spiders and scorpions,' Ricketts said. 'Like we did in Oman.'

'I preferred it there,' Lampton said. 'It wasn't a rat's maze of backstreets. It was all out in the open and the enemy couldn't be mistaken. He might pop up from behind a rock, but you knew you could shoot at him without being grilled by the green slime or the RUC CID.'

'Right,' Jock said. 'As our Army sergeant told us, here you're fighting children, teenagers and screaming women, as well as the IRA. Not good, folks. Not helpful.'

'Still,' Gumboot said, 'a man could make a good bit of money on the side here. As Sergeant Lovelock kindly informed us, the whole city's run on graft and protection rackets, so we could form our own little syndicate.'

'Right,' Martin said, beginning to enjoy the sort of banter they always referred to as bullshit. 'We offer protection from the Catholics *and* the Prods.'

'Arrest them, then ask for a hand-out to let the poor bastards go again. That should rake in the shekels!'

'You think it's funny,' Lampton said, 'but this place can corrupt anyone. When the SAS first came here two of them, obviously thinking the whole place was lawless, attempted to rob a bank in Londonderry.'

'I don't believe it!' Taff exclaimed.

'It's true,' Ricketts told him. 'Both of them got six years in prison and the SAS got a reputation it didn't want.'

'I mean, to attempt to rob a bank and then *fail*,' Jock said in disgust. 'They must have been crap-hats.'

Young Danny glanced at Dead-eye Dick, who was silently downing a pint at the bar. 'He's really quiet,' Danny said.

'Just like you,' Martin said.

'He's a cold-blooded killer,' Jock said, 'who requires a wide berth. You remember that bastard in Oman, Gumboot? He was one weird companion!'

'Right,' Gumboot replied. 'Always dressed up in Arab clothes and running around with the *firqats*. They say he is as good with a knife as he is with his rifle.'

Danny stared admiringly at Parker, then gave a slight smile. 'A good soldier,' he said.

'He is that,' Ricketts told him, knowing that Danny admired the silent Dead-eye because the youngster, even in Continuation Training, had shown all the hallmarks of being just like him – a natural fighter and possibly a born killer, baby face or not. Ricketts checked his watch. 'OK, men,' he said. 'Time to go. The Head Sheds await us.'

Some of the men groaned melodramatically, but they finished their drinks, then filed out of the canteen to go to the briefing room.

While the others were leaving, Danny went up to Dead-eye, tapped him on the shoulder, and spoke to him, telling him that the late-night briefing was about to begin. Dead-eye stared stonily at him, then nodded and waved him away. Danny grinned shyly at Ricketts as he left, then Dead-eye finished his drink, slid off the stool and walked up to Ricketts and Lampton.

'Seems like a good kid,' he said.

'Not bad,' Lampton replied.

Dead-eye just nodded.

Outside, in the freezing night air, they hurriedly crossed a stretch of wind-blown ground to the Portakabin used as a briefing room. Mercifully, it was bright and warm inside. Most of the men were already seated, so Ricketts and Lampton sat in the back row. The Head Sheds on the dais, in front of the blackboard, were Captain Dubois and Lieutenant Cranfield, both back in uniform. As before, Sergeant Lovelock was sitting at a desk beside them, guarding another pile of manila folders.

'Evening, gentlemen,' Lieutenant Cranfield said. 'I trust you're all in good spirits.'

'We'd feel better if we were back in the bar, boss,' Jock replied.

Cranfield just grinned. 'You'll have time for one more before closing,' he said. 'Then you have to be good boys. So! Why this emergency, late-night briefing?'

'Do tell us, boss!' Lampton responded.

After glancing automatically at the sombre Captain Dubois, Cranfield turned back to his men. 'The first thing I should say is that you twelve are here only as an advance party. In a few weeks the whole of D Squadron, numbering seventy-five men, is going to be shipped in, but in the meantime you have to carry the load – and over the next couple of weeks that could become rather heavy.'

'Then give it to the British Army,' Gumboot said. 'They're all brawn and no brains.'

Captain Dubois flushed, then managed a tight grin. Cranfield, whose grin was more genuine, waited until the laughter had died down before continuing: 'The second thing I should tell you is that we're not just here for routine patrols. Our brief is to cleanse Belfast and south Armagh of the IRA – completely, once and for all.'

When the surprised murmuring had subsided, Sergeant Lampton said: 'That sounds pretty ambitious, boss.'

'Ambitious, but not impossible. I feel that we're now in a position to poke a hole in the dam wall, then split it wide open. We have some of the most important IRA men in our sights and we're going to take them out. When we've done so, we'll have dealt a decisive blow to their morale and won ourselves a propaganda victory of such dimensions that it could turn the tide wholly in our favour.'

'Just how important are these men, boss?' Ricketts asked. 'And who are they, exactly?'

'We have reason to believe they're the four-man PIRA active service unit that recently topped ten of our best sources.'

Ricketts glanced quizzically at Sergeant Lovelock, who offered a slight, knowing grin. Then Ricketts returned his gaze to Lieutenant Cranfield. 'Is it true that those deaths may have been the cause of Corporal Phillips's suicide?'

'This subject was raised at the last briefing, Sergeant, but it's still not up for discussion. The reason for Corporal Phillips's suicide remains unknown, though we assume it was stress. I'm not at liberty, however, to discuss the work he was doing.' He nodded at Sergeant Lovelock, who stood up, walked around his desk, and distributed the manila folders to all the troopers. 'The men we're after,' Cranfield said, 'are PIRA members Michael Quinn, Patrick Mulgrew, Seamus McGrath and John Houlihan. You'll find photos of them in those folders, along with intelligence reports on each individual. Quinn is the leader of this four-man ASU. Our job is to take them out as soon as possible.'

'And put them in Long Kesh?' Lampton asked.

'No,' Cranfield said, taking a deep breath and slowly letting it out again. 'Our job is to cancel them completely without breaking the law.'

The men glanced at one another, surprised. Some of them tried to cover their discomfort at the silence by studying the photographs in the folders. Eventually Parker broke the silence in his customary flat tones: 'What's the strategy, boss?'

'For this operation,' Captain Dubois said, 'you men are going to be kitted out tomorrow. At dawn the day after, the army is going to do a cordon-and-search sweep of the lower Falls Road, with particular emphasis on the street where Michael Quinn lives. Quite deliberately, we're going to make this sweep more thorough than most, using hundreds of troops and making a great show of searching every house – after throwing their occupants temporarily out into the street and frisking the men on the pavements, in full view of their wives and kids. While all this is going on, causing a great deal of confusion, a four-man SAS team will take over the attic of the house of one of our touts, located directly opposite Quinn's place. At the same time, army surveillance specialists will be planting miniaturized audio and video recording devices in Quinn's house.'

'Why not just place the OP in Quinn's attic?' Jock asked.

'Because Quinn's a hard man, very experienced, and that's the first place he'll check when we leave. Nor can we bug his phone in the ordinary manner. But he won't think to look for other miniaturized surveillance devices, some of which will be interacting with the surveillance equipment in the OP across the street.'

'Understood, boss,' Jock said. 'What about the rest of us? The remaining eight.'

'Quinn has a country cottage in south Armagh,' Cranfield said, 'not far from here, close to the border. While the covert OP is keeping tabs on his comings and goings in the Falls, including what's said and done inside his house, the remaining eight men will do the same in two rural OPs located near the cottage – one overlooking the road between the cottage and Belfast, the other on the road that leads to Dublin.'

'For what purpose?' Martin asked naïvely.

'Both the cottage and the house in the Falls Road are used for Quinn's ASU meetings. Based on information received from the three OPs regarding his plans and movements, we'll decide just when and where to take him and the other three out. It has to be both lawful and highly public, so the time and place must be right. Any questions?'

'Yes, boss,' Ricketts said. 'Who does what?'

'You'll be told that tomorrow morning when you report to the Quartermaster's stores after breakfast. The rest of the day will be spent on weapons testing, familiarization with the surveillance equipment, and general instructions regarding, in particular, the urban OP. A final weapons and kit inspection will be made tomorrow night, immediately after dinner. After the inspection, no one will be allowed to drink or even visit the NAAFI canteen for any reason.' When the moans and groans had died away, Cranfield asked: 'Any more questions?'

'Yes, boss,' Gumboot said. 'If we're not allowed to drink tomorrow, can we go and get pissed right now?'

'It's your last chance, trooper. Just make sure you put those folders in your lockers before you go out. Also make sure you thoroughly acquaint yourselves with their contents by tomorrow evening. Right? Class dismissed!'

Leaving the briefing room, the men returned to their bashas, where they locked the manila folders in their lockers, then hurried out for a few more pints in the NAAFI canteen.

8

Saracen armoured cars, armoured troop carriers, or 'pigs', and RUC paddy-wagons penetrated the lower Falls, headlights beaming into the morning darkness like the flaring eyes of prehistoric beasts. The convoy rumbled ominously past police stations and army barricades along the Falls Road without interference, then broke up into separate columns that turned into three parallel side streets to begin the early morning cordon-and-search sweep. Within minutes the area was surrounded and the three streets were blocked off.

His attention drawn not by the rumble of the advancing vehicles, but by an approaching helicopter, a dicker looked up, saw what was happening, and shouted a warning, his youthful voice echoing eerily in the silence.

Almost immediately, his mates materialized out of dark doorways and narrow, littered alleys of torture and death to add their bellowed warnings to his own.

Even as sleepy citizens started opening their front

doors, many still in their nightwear, British Army and Parachute Regiment troops poured out of the armoured pigs, into dark streets streaked with morning light. Wearing DPM clothing and helmets, but bulked out even more with ArmourShield General Purpose Vests, or GPVs, including ceramic contoured plates, fragmentation vests, and groin panels, they looked like invaders from space. Even worse, they were armed with sledgehammers, SA-80 assault rifles, and Heckler & Koch MP5 sub-machine-guns – the latter particularly effective for use in confined spaces. Others, the 'snatch' teams, there to take in the prisoners, looked just as fearsome in full riot gear, including shields and truncheons.

RUC officers trained at the SAS Counter Revolutionary Warfare Wing at Hereford, wearing flak jackets and carrying either 5.56mm Ruger Mini-14 assault rifles or batons, jumped out of the back of the paddy-wagons and surrounded their vehicles as the soldiers and paratroopers raced in opposite directions along the street, hammering on doors with the butts of their weapons and bawling for the people to come out.

British Army snipers clambered up on to the roofs from lightweight aluminium assault ladders and from there gave cover with Lee Enfield .303-inch sniper rifles. Wearing earphones, they would be warned of any likely trouble spots either by officers on the street or by the Royal Marine Gazelle observation helicopter that was now hovering right above the rooftops, its spinning rotors creating a fierce wind that blew the rubbish in the gutters across the street.

'Get out, you Fenian bastards! On the pavement!'

When Lampton, Ricketts, Gumboot and Taff looked out through the half-open doors of their Saracen, they saw the soldiers roughly pushing angry women and dazed children aside to grab their menfolk and haul them out on to the pavement. Other soldiers were forcing their way inside the houses to begin what would almost certainly be damaging searches of the premises. When front doors were not opened on request, the soldiers with the sledgehammers smashed them open. As the older male residents of the street, most still in pyjamas, were pushed face first against the wall and made to spread their hands and legs for rough frisking, women screamed abuse, children either did the same or burst into tears, and the youthful dickers further along the street hurled stones, lumps of concrete and abuse.

'Shit!' Gumboot burst out inside the safety of the Saracen. 'I thought this was supposed to be a fake raid, just put on for our benefit.'

'They have to make it look real,' Lampton informed him, 'so the only soldiers who know about us are the ones taking us into O'Leary's house. This is the real thing, Gumboot.'

'Bloody nasty,' Taff said.

'Right,' Gumboot replied. 'Those soldiers are acting like fucking thugs.'

'It's because they're frightened,' Taff said. 'They haven't the time for consideration. They can't avoid the women and children, the enemy could be anyone, some of the houses could be booby-trapped, one of the dickers might have a gun – and so on.'

'Right,' Frank Lampton said. 'In this kind of situation you could get shot in the back by an invalid in his bed, stabbed in the stomach by a housewife with a breadknife, or blown up by a booby-trapped bathroom door – you just never know. So their only thought is to get in and out as quickly as possible and to hell with the rest of it.'

'That's why they smash the doors down and tear the houses apart,' Ricketts said. 'They're not gonna hang about being polite or helping to rearrange the furniture afterwards. They go in, take the house apart and leave. It's not nice, but it works.'

Looking out of the Saracen, they saw two of the soldiers grab a suspect in pyjamas, haul him away from the wall where he had been frisked, and push him roughly into the centre of the road, where an RUC guard hit him with a truncheon and forced him up into a paddy-wagon. A single shot rang out, followed immediately by the sound of breaking glass.

'Mick bastard!' a soldier bawled as he cracked a man's head with the butt of his SA-80, making him

topple back and drop the pistol he'd just fired wildly in the air, doing damage only to a window.

When he straightened up, the man turned out to be no more than a teenager. He removed his hand from his temple and looked in amazement at the blood on his fingers, before being jerked sideways by the soldier, then kicked brutally towards the RUC officer, who drove him up into the paddy-wagon like someone using an electric prod on a cow.

'Get in there, you murdering Fenian bastard!' the RUC man exploded, giving the youth a last blow with the truncheon as he stumbled into the vehicle. Elsewhere, soldiers with riot shields were herding groups of men against the wall and using truncheons to force their legs apart.

'Hands against the wall!' one soldier was bawling. 'Spread those fucking legs! Now don't make a move!'

As other soldiers poured in and out of houses, sometimes smashing their way in with sledge-hammers, housewives in curlers screamed abuse and attacked them with their fists, children ran about like wild animals, some laughing, some crying, and the dickers further along the road kept throwing stones and lumps of concrete at the line of soldiers forming a cordon of riot shields across the street.

Just as another couple of men were prodded up into the paddy-wagon visible outside the Saracen,

Sergeant Lovelock appeared at the half-open doors with a group of paratroopers behind him. 'OK,' he said, waving his right hand. 'Out you get. Half of your kit's already been taken in and we've no time to waste.'

The four-man SAS OP team climbed out of the Saracen. Like most of the regular Army troops, they were wearing DPM clothing, but with camouflaged soft combat caps instead of helmets, and leather and Gore-tex Danner boots instead of standard-issue British Army boots. They did not have their bergens, as these would have been spotted instantly, so were carrying only what kit they could manage on their belts, in their pockets and in their hands. This included fourteen days' high-calorie rations, mostly chocolate and sweets, on the basis of two days per one day's ration. In bivvy bags on their belts they carried spare underwear and a first-aid kit; and, also on the belt, flashlights and binoculars. They carried as well extra ammunition for the only weapons they were allowed on this operation: their standard-issue 9mm Browning High Power handguns and the short 9mm Sterling Mk 5 sub-machine-gun with retractable butt and 34-round magazines, which they were now carrying openly.

However, as this equipment was insufficient for a lengthy urban recce, the rest of their kit was being carried to the OP by an escort patrol of paratroopers. Some had already entered the house opposite and were making their way slowly along

the single loft space of the terrace to O'Leary's loft, located right opposite Quinn's house. Those men, and some of the paratroopers, were taking the rest of the kit, including water in plastic bottles; spare radio batteries; medical packs; extra ammunition; 35mm cameras and rolls of film; tape-recorders; thermal imagers and night-vision scopes; an advanced laser audio surveillance transceiver; brown, plastic-backed notebooks and ballpens; sleeping bags; packs of moisturized cloths for cleaning their faces and hands; towels; toilet paper; and sealable plastic bags for their excrement and urine.

'Let's go!' Lovelock said.

Protected by the ring of heavily armed para-troopers, half deafened by the roaring of the helicopter hovering directly above them, Ricketts, Lampton, Gumboot and Taff raced across the road, through bawling RUC officers and watchful soldiers, past Saracens and pigs, up on to the pavement on the opposite side. There, while British Army soldiers dragged reluctant men and women out of their homes, the paratroopers pushed their way into one of the houses. Once inside, a couple of them proceeded to 'search' the place by noisily sweeping ornaments and bric-à-brac off tables and cupboards, removing drawers and tipping their contents on to the floor, and generally smashing the place up. Meanwhile, the others led the four SAS men upstairs to the trapdoor already opened in the floor of the loft.

Forming his hands into a stirrup, a hefty paratrooper said, 'OK, up you get.' One by one, the four SAS men placed a foot in his joined hands and were hoisted up into the dark loft. The rest of the paratroopers followed suit, leaving only the big one standing below the trapdoor, surrounded by the rest of the kit required for the OP. While the paratroopers on the ground floor continued to wreck the house by way of searching it, the big paratrooper below the trapdoor handed up the kit piece by piece. When it was all in the loft, the men divided it between them and then 'mouse-holed' their way along the terrace, practically the whole length of the street, until they met up with the others already in the cramped space in O'Leary's roof.

'This is it,' Sergeant Lovelock said as the paratroopers laid the rest of the kit and equipment down around the edges of the loft space. 'And there's your peep-hole.' He pointed to where a slate nail in the roof had been removed and replaced with a rubber band that allowed the slate to be raised and lowered, thus providing a spy-hole for the naked eye, binoculars, cameras or thermal imagers. 'At this moment one of our specialists is placing a miniature surveillance probe near the ceiling of the adjoining wall in the house next door to Quinn's without the occupants knowing a thing. That, combined with your advanced laser

128

system, should enable you to hear, see and record everything that goes on in Quinn's place. Any questions?'

'No,' Sergeant Lampton said.

'OK. We've got to go now. Good luck.'

Lovelock patted Lampton on the shoulder, then, using a hand signal, ordered the paratroopers to follow him back along the terrace to the open trapdoor by which they had entered. This they did, dropping down one by one through the small, square hole until they had all disappeared. When the last of them had gone, Ricketts, who had followed them this far, replaced the trapdoor, checked that it was secure, then returned to join the others above O'Leary's house.

Lampton was looking through the peep-hole.

'What's happening?' Ricketts asked.

'They've got Michael Quinn out on the pavement and he's going apeshit. The soldiers have just left the house next door, so the probe must be planted. I think the Army will start pulling out now, taking a few prisoners with them for show. Yep, they've just taken Quinn. They'll pretend they came here to get him. They'll take him to Castlereagh, put him through the wringer, then eventually release him and let him come home, thinking he's fooled them again. I don't think he'll even check his own loft. He seems to think this is genuine. The fact that they've also arrested the tout who owns this place will make the raid seem even more genuine.' He turned away from the peep-hole and motioned Ricketts over. 'Here, take a look.'

'Start unpacking this gear,' Ricketts said to Gumboot and Taff. 'And remember that from this moment on we have to be quiet as mice.'

'I thought it was the tout's house,' Taff said.

'It is, which is certainly a help, but loud noises could be heard in the adjoining houses, so we have to keep it down.' He glanced at the adjoining loft to the right and said, 'That's going to be your bog, so be particularly quiet there, as it belongs to the house next door.' Catching Lampton's grin, he went to the peep-hole, raised the slate and looked down on the street.

The hard man he recognized from the intelligence photo as Michael Quinn was struggling vigorously and bawling abuse as two soldiers with truncheons dragged him off the pavement and forced him up into one of the RUC paddy-wagons. At the same time, another man, whom Ricketts suspected was the tout, was being half-dragged from the area directly below the loft to be thrown into the same vehicle.

That, Ricketts reasoned, was a good idea, as the tout would now appear to be one of those high on the Brits' wanted list. It would make him look good in the eyes of his mates and neighbours, including Quinn.

When the doors of the paddy-wagon had been slammed shut on Quinn and the tout, the house-wives and children on the pavements bawled even more abuse at the soldiers and RUC officers. The latter, however, were already getting back into their vehicles and the engines were roaring into life.

As the first of the Saracens and pigs moved off along the street, an even louder roaring came from directly above the house. Looking up as high as he could through the peep-hole, Ricketts saw the Gazelle observation helicopter flying directly overhead, heading back to Armagh. By the time it had disappeared beyond row upon row of rooftops, the last of the Saracens, pigs and paddy-wagons had also disappeared from below, leaving the street to the irate or shocked inhabitants.

Some of the women hurried into their houses, only to rush out again, complaining tearfully about the devastation inside.

Disturbed by that sight, Ricketts dropped the slate back over the peep-hole and turned back to face the other three in the loft. Gumboot and Taff had already unpacked a lot of the kit and were balefully examining the plastic bags intended for their own shit and piss. Lampton, meanwhile, was opening the tripod for the audio surveillance transceiver.

'Take off your boots,' he told them as he unfolded

the tripod, 'and don't put them on again until we leave this place.'

'Home sweet home,' Ricketts murmured, gazing around the dark, freezing, cobwebbed loft.

'I've lived in worse,' Gumboot said.

9

That evening, close to midnight, with the covert OP already established opposite Michael Quinn's house in Belfast, Sergeant 'Dead-eye Dick' Parker and Troopers Jock McGregor, Danny 'Baby Face' Porter and Martin Renshaw, were driven out of Bessbrook in a dark-blue high-sided van to set up a second covert OP overlooking Quinn's weekend home in the 'bandit country' of south Armagh.

Though normally the overt OPs were manned and resupped by helicopter, this one would be left alone during its existence and was being set up in strict secrecy. The van, therefore, was being driven by a British Army REME corporal in civilian clothing, guarded by a crack marksman paratrooper, also wearing normal clothes. The OP's SAS team, on the other hand, were wearing DPM windproof clothing, Danner boots with Gore-tex lining, and soft, peaked, camouflaged combat caps. The exposed parts of their faces, necks and hands were smeared with stick camouflage, suitable for blending in with local foliage.

Stopped repeatedly by Army roadblocks, the men in the van had to show their IDs, which in this case were genuine. They were always then allowed to proceed. Nevertheless, the many stops slowed them down considerably and it was just after two in the morning when they finally reached their destination.

Quinn's weekend house was in rolling farmlands in Kilevy, surrounded by the hills along the A1 and high enough to afford a glimpse of Carlingford Lough and the Irish Sea. When the REME corporal parked the van and switched off his headlights in a pitch-black winding lane near Kilevy, the men hurriedly climbed out, with Dead-eye Dick, Jock, the paratrooper and the REME driver going into all-round defence as Martin and Danny unloaded the equipment.

No one spoke.

When the unloading was completed, the four SAS men strapped on their heavily laden bergens, distributed the rest of the equipment between them, then clambered over a fence to begin the long march up a dark, windswept, grassy hill. As they did so, the REME driver, still protected by the paratrooper, turned the van around and headed back to Bessbrook.

The men marching uphill were heavily burdened indeed, with overpacked bergens weighing over fifty pounds and the rest of their weapons, ammunition, equipment, water and rations, either fixed to their webbing or carried by hand, thus making an even greater burden. As the weapons included a GPMG, a couple of L42A1 Lee Enfield .303 bolt-action sniper rifles with starlight 'scopes, M16 assault rifles with M203 grenade launchers, and two 5.56mm Colt Commando semi-automatics with 30-round box magazines, and as the equipment included various surveillance systems and recording machines, as well as a PRC 319 radio, it was a daunting load to carry for any distance.

'Donkey soldiers,' Jock whispered to Martin. 'That's what the *firqats* called us in Oman and that's what we are now. Bloody donkeys!'

Martin tried to laugh, but was so breathless he nearly choked, so instead maintained silence.

Ordered apart by Sergeant 'Dead-eye Dick' Parker, the men advanced up the hill in a well-spaced line, with Jock out front as 'point' man, or lead scout, Danny and Martin in the middle to cover both flanks, and Dead-eye bringing up the rear as 'Tail-end Charlie'. They made it to the OP by a zigzagging route that took in a series of pre-designated RVs, or rendezvous points: the gate of a fence, a copse of trees, a particular hill. Though this took up more time, it was a vital part of their anti-ambush tactics. Eventually, however, after a final rendezvous, or FRV, during which they checked the map with the aid of a pencil torch, they arrived at the location chosen for the OP.

'OK,' Dead-eye Dick, the Patrol Commander,

said, lowering his own heavy loads to the ground. 'This is where we dig in.'

The location was the windy summit of a hill with a glimpse of the lough and sea on one side and, on the other, an unobstructed view of Quinn's cottage – necessary not only for eyeball recces, but for the line-of-sight path required for the laser surveillance system. The location had also been chosen because it was on the direct line of a hedgerow that snaked over the crest of the hill and could be used as the protective wall of the OP.

The clouds were low and patchy, showing stars between, and moonlight made strips of sea glint occasionally in the distance. The wind was cold and strong, howling like a banshee, and frost glinted here and there on the grassy ground.

While the other men sorted out their kit, Jock used the PRC 319 to establish communications with the base at Bessbrook. Having confirmed that the OP had 'comms', or communications, from this location, Dead-eye took guard and radio watch, leaving the experienced Jock, with the help of Danny and Martin, to prepare the OP.

While it was unlikely that they would be seen by enemy aircraft, of which there were none, it was possible that a British Army helicopter crew, not knowing of their mission, would mistake them for a PIRA murder squad. For this reason, the first thing they did was put up a hessian screen, with a poncho and camouflage net for overhead

cover, supported on wooden stakes, looped at one end over the hedgerow, and held down with iron pickets and rope.

Once this basic form of protection had been raised, the three men used spades and pickaxes to dig out a large rectangular area suitable for a long-term, top-to-tail OP, with one end running under the hedgerow.

Four shallow 'scrapes' were then dug in the main scrape: one for the observer, one for the sentry, and two as 'rest bays'. One of the latter was for the man having a proper sleep in a sleeping bag; the other was for the man resting from guard or observation duties while taking care of his personal administration matters – such as jotting down his observations – or perhaps just having a snack and a rest while remaining awake.

A fifth shallow scrape was dug out of the middle of the triangular OP as a 'kit-well' for water, high-calorie foods, weapons, spare ammunition, batteries, toiletries and other equipment.

The soil from the scrapes was scattered around the ground a good distance away from the OP. The hessian-and-net covering of the OP was then covered in grass, gorse and vegetation torn from the hedgerow.

A camouflaged entry/exit hole was made in the hessian hanging to the ground at the rear end of the OP. Last, but most important, a camouflaged rectangular viewing hole was shaped from the hedgerow and hessian covering the side of the OP overlooking the target – in this case Quinn's cottage and the road passing it, located about 150 metres away, across the road at the bottom of the hill.

With the OP completed, the rest of the equipment was unpacked and prepared for use.

It was now that the newcomer, Martin Renshaw, came into his own. A former electrical research engineer with Marconi, then with the Pilatus Britten-Norman experimental aircraft production company in the Isle of Wight, Martin had joined the army specifically to get into the Royal Corps of Signals and, through that regiment, into the SAS. Immediately after being badged by the latter, he had spent six weeks each at the Hereford and Royal Signals establishments at Catterick and Blandford, where he had learned about the special surveillance requirements of the SAS, with particular regard to Counter-Terrorist (CT) operations in Northern Ireland. He was therefore particularly thrilled to be here at last and about to put all his training to work.

'Let's see what you can do, kid,' Dead-eye said. 'You can play with your toys now.'

The tripod which Martin set up in front of the viewing hole overlooking Quinn's house was not for the GPMG, which would only be used in dire emergency, but for the cumbersome Thorn EMI multi-role thermal imager, including an infrared capability. Looking like an exceptionally large

video camera, it could scan outside walls, track body heat, and reveal the position of those inside the building, by day or by night, in smoke or fog.

'If he leaves the room,' Martin said, 'we're all going to know it.'

Complementing the large, tripod-mounted thermal imager were two other items of highly advanced equipment.

Photographs of those entering or leaving Quinn's cottage, whether by day or by night, would be taken with a Davin Optical Modulux image intensifier connected to a Nikon 35mm SLR camera with interchangeable long-distance and binocular lenses.

'It can also be used as a night sight,' Martin explained enthusiastically, 'but it only works in the visible spectrum and its effectiveness is reduced by smoke, fog, and even dense foliage. Nevertheless, for our long-distance, day and night photographic needs it can't really be bettered.'

He also set up a Hawkeye Systems Model HT10 thermal imaging camera capable of detecting men and vehicles at long distances, either in low light or in total darkness, while producing high-quality video pictures with up to seven times magnification. While the thermal picture was displayed automatically on an integral video monitor for direct viewing, it could also be displayed on a separate monitor for remote applications, such as recording for later visual analysis.

'What the hell's that?' Jock asked Martin, when the latter set up two more tripods and fixed what looked like complicated transmitters, or recording devices, to them.

Camouflaged in hessian, the end of the camera-shaped object was poking through the viewing hole. The other object, which looked like a radio receiver, was joined to the first by a complex web of electric cables.

'It's an STG laser surveillance system,' Martin said as he made his adjustments.

'What the fuck's STG?'

'Surveillance Technology Group.'

'So that's a laser gun?'

'No, not a gun. It's a laser surveillance transmitter. We'll use it to record conversations in Quinn's place and transmit them back here. I'm setting the transmitter on what's known as a line-of-sight path to the cottage, to direct an invisible beam on to the front window.'

'An invisible beam?' Jock asked sceptically.

'Yes. Imagine the window as the diaphragm of a microphone with oscillating sound waves. The invisible beam bounces off the window, back to the optical receiver in our OP. The receiver then converts the modulated beam into audio signals, which in turn are filtered, amplified and converted into clear conversation. The conversation can then be monitored through headphones and simultaneously recorded on a tape-recorder. Pretty neat, eh?'

'Fucking *Star Wars*,' Jock said. 'Anything to help us see in the dark if those PIRA fuckers try to take us by surprise?'

'Yes,' Martin said, now in his element and enjoying himself. 'We've got a hand-held thermal imager operating on SWIR – that's short-wavelength infrared. Also, a little number called "Iris", which is an infrared intruder-detection system, remote controlled and effective over up to five kilometres. Each of the two men on guard will have one or the other of those to give them an extra set of eyes and ears.'

'I'm going right back to my childhood,' Jock said. 'Fucking *Flash Gordon*.'

'That was long before your childhood,' Danny told him, 'even though you *do* look that age.'

'Fuck you, kid,' Jock said.

Finally, when the surveillance equipment was set up, Dead-eye took a couple of brown, plastic-backed 'bingo' books out of his bergen and laid them on the ground below the viewing hole, beside the legs of the tripods. Already containing the names of wanted men, missing vehicles and suspected addresses, the notebooks would soon also contain details of everything seen and heard during this lengthy recce.

Dead-eye turned away from the viewing hole and looked directly at Martin.

'Are you ready?' he asked in his curiously chilling monotone.

'Yes,' Martin said.

'OK.' Dead-eye fixed his gaze on Jock and Danny. 'You two stay here. We're going down to Quinn's house, but we'll be back in about an hour. If any of these instruments indicate that someone's coming, check that it's us before you open fire and blow our nuts off.'

'Will do!' Jock chirped. 'But why are you going to Quinn's house at this hour of the morning?'

'We only have coverage of the front of Quinn's place,' Dead-eye explained, 'so while the bastard's being held in Castlereagh detention barracks, this electrical wizard, Trooper Renshaw, is going to plant miniaturized bugs at the side and rear of the cottage. Don't ask me how.'

Before anyone could say anything else, Dead-eye picked up a 5.56mm Colt Commando semi-automatic and a couple of 30-round box magazines, then crawled out of the OP. Seeing him go, Martin hurriedly took an olive-green canvas shoulder bag from the kit-well, slung it over his right shoulder, picked up an M16 assault rifle, then followed him out.

It was still dark and cold outside, with the wind howling across the fields, but they made their way rapidly, carefully, down the hill until they reached the road running past the cottage. After glancing left and right to check that no vehicles were coming, they crossed the road, opened the garden gate, closed it carefully behind them,

then hurried up the path, stopping near the front door.

Dead-eye glanced left and right, then cocked his head as if listening. 'No dogs,' he whispered. When Martin nodded his agreement, Dead-eye led him around the side of the cottage and stopped by the kitchen window.

'Here?'

'Yes,' Martin said.

While Dead-eye kept watch with the Colt Commando crooked in his left forearm, in what is known as the Belfast Cradle, Martin found a stepladder in the back garden, placed it against the wall by the window, climbed it, then used a small hand drill to quietly bore a hole through the top of the wooden window frame. When this was done, he pushed a fibre-optic probe camera, less than an eighth of an inch thick, through the hole, fixed its wired end to the outside of the window frame, then attached a miniaturized transmitter to the frame, right next to the probe, and wired the probe to it. Though it would have been visible to a keen eye, it was unlikely that anyone not deliberately looking would see either the tiny probe or the small transmitter.

'One more,' Martin said. Removing the stepladder from the wall and carrying it around to the back of the house, he placed it over the window of what appeared to be a rear living room and fixed another probe and transmitter to the top of the wooden frame. When the job was completed, he returned the ladder to where he had found it and carefully checked that nothing else had been disturbed. Satisfied, he glanced once more at his handiwork, then said: 'OK. The laser surveillance system in the OP will pick up from the front room, the probe in the side will pick up from the kitchen, and the probe at the back will pick up from the other living room. That should just about do it.'

'The bedrooms and the bog?' Dead-eye asked without a flicker of irony.

'We can't have everything,' Martin replied with a broad grin. 'Come on, boss, let's get out of here.'

With Dead-eye again in the lead and still cradling his Colt Commando, they crossed the road and made their way back up the dark hill. A good distance away from the OP, but within speaking range, they stopped and identified themselves, each personally announcing his own presence for voice identification. Given Jock's permission to continue, they made their way up to the summit, slipped through a space in the hedgerow, dropped on to their hands and knees, then crawled breathlessly back into the OP.

'All done,' Dead-eye said. 'Now let's wait for that Irish bastard to come calling.'

Coins were tossed to see who would take first watch. Dead-eye and Danny lost the toss, allowing Jock and Martin to crawl gratefully into the scrapes and catch up on lost sleep.

The OP overlooking Quinn's cottage on the stretch of road that ran to and from Belfast was now a functioning unit. At approximately the same time, as they all knew, a third covert OP was being set up, also overlooking the cottage, but further south, to cover the road leading to Dublin.

Whichever direction Quinn decided to travel in, they had him well covered.

10

Life in O'Leary's loft was not very comfortable. By the end of the first day the men realized just how uncomfortable it was; by the end of the first night they felt tired, dirty and cramped, with nerves already stretched to the limit and humiliation added to their general sense of deprivation. By day three they felt grubby, exhausted, claustrophobic and increasingly tense.

It was cold, too. Outside, when they looked through the peep-hole, they could see frost on the pavements and an occasional snow shower. The Belfast winds howled bitterly. In the loft, because of the need to be quiet and not let O'Leary's neighbours suspect their presence, they could not wear their boots and so, though they wore extra layers of socks, their feet were constantly freezing and their bodies, likewise wrapped in extra clothing, nonetheless were cold more often than not.

The main problems, however, were domestic. No food could be cooked, so they were forced to subsist on dry, high-calorie rations, such as biscuits, cheese, chocolate and sweets. Although they had a couple of vacuum flasks of hot tea and coffee, they had to strictly limit themselves to one hot drink a day and, for the rest of the time, drink tepid water from the plastic water bottles. As there was nowhere to wash, they could only clean themselves with moisturized cloths and clean their teeth, or rather freshen their mouths, with chewing gum. Even worse, as the loft of O'Leary's house was not divided from the other lofts, the loft space of the adjoining house was designated as a toilet, with the men using plastic bags for this purpose; which they had to seal and store carefully after use. Since they also had to do this in full view of the other men, Taff found it to be particularly humiliating.

'I was prepared for anything when I was badged,' he whispered, 'except for shitting into plastic bags in front of the other men. I mean, that's too much for me.'

'You've got an anal complex,' Gumboot replied. 'Me? I'll shit anywhere except in my own pants and I don't mind who sees me doing it. A shit is a shit, mate.'

'You're bloody disgusting, Gumboot. I put it down to country living. I've heard a lot of stories about life on the farm and none of them were very nice. Carnal knowledge with animals and suchlike. Did you ever do that?'

'A hole is a hole,' Gumboot said. 'What do *you* think, old mate?'

Taff didn't know what to think. He was too tired to think. They had to sleep sitting upright, against the brick walls of the loft, a blanket wrapped around them for warmth, a cushion under the arse. They rested two at a time, with one sleeping, one just relaxing, though the second was compelled to keep his eye on the first in case he talked or cried out in his sleep, alerting the neighbours on either side of O'Leary.

For that reason, no matter how tired they were, they were all too tense to sleep properly.

'That fucking O'Leary sleeps better than we do,' Lampton said sardonically to Ricketts. 'I could kill for his bed.'

They had learnt from their own surveillance that the tout's name was O'Leary and that he had been released from Castlereagh detention barracks at the same time as Quinn. They knew he had returned to the house because they could hear him moving about below. Of course, he knew they were above him and tried to stay as quiet as possible, but they heard practically everything – his radio and TV, the flushing of his toilet, the opening and shutting of doors, drawers and cupboards, conversations with his unwanted visitors – and this, combined with what they were picking up from the surveillance, rendered what he did below to be entirely superfluous.

More interesting what was O'Leary had done before for Lieutenant Cranfield.

'The more I hear, the more I fear for him,' Lampton said. 'Cranfield's out on a narrow ledge.'

The surveillance was a welcome distraction from the oppressive horrors of daily life in the loft, which inhibited movement and forced them to be unnaturally quiet, talking only in whispers. The surveillance, therefore, was a form of work that acted as therapy and also contained its own fascination, which revolved around Lieutenant Cranfield, who was increasingly revealed as a man unlike other SAS officers.

'He thinks he's playing an exciting game,' Ricketts said, 'but he's going to get into trouble and maybe drag us down with him.'

Since starting the surveillance, Ricketts and Lampton in particular, perhaps with a clearer picture of what was actually going on, felt that they were being sucked into a whirlpool of Cranfield's making. The surveillance itself, apart from being a distraction from the rigours of the loft, was a seductive business, drawing them out of themselves and into the world of Michael Quinn and his fellow PIRA members.

Hidden in the loft, seeing Quinn's world through the peep-hole, concentrated and magnified, as it were, by the use of the Thorn EMI hand-held thermal imager, weighing only five kilograms, which he carried on a string around his neck, Ricketts soon began to feel that he was more familiar with Quinn's world than he was with his own. This sense of extraordinary intimacy, of dissolving into someone else's existence, was only increased by his frequent recourse to the camera, which was a 35mm Nikon F3HP with a heavy-duty titanium body, telescopic lens, and a Davis Minimodulux image intensifier also used as a night-vision scope. Ricketts had taken so many photos, and studied Quinn so many times through the viewfinder of the camera, seeing him magnified, his every blemish exposed, his every magnified, exaggerated, that he sometimes felt that he sion actually becoming the Irishman himself.

Perhaps, Ricketts reasoned, Lieutenant Cranfield hadn't considered just how detailed the surveillance of Quinn could be and, therefore, just how much about himself it would reveal.

'He killed O'Halloran all right,' Ricketts said to Lampton when they had listened to yet another conversation picked up by the tiny fibre-optic probe camera which had been inserted near the ceiling of the wall in the adjoining house when the soldiers were pretending to search it. With its advanced laser system, the tiny probe picked up the minute vibrations created by conversations in Quinn's place and transmitted them to a tape-recorder in O'Leary's loft, thus giving Ricketts and Lampton an invaluable but increasingly hair-raising glimpse into the world of the terrorists and their hunters.

Released from Castlereagh, Quinn had returned to his home and called an immediate meeting with the other three members of his PIRA murder squad. During that meeting, every word of which was picked up by the probe, Quinn confirmed that Captain Dubois and Lieutenant Cranfield together had made numerous illegal trips across the border in Eire to snatch wanted IRA men and bring them back to Northern Ireland to be 'captured' by the RUC and imprisoned. Because of this, it was widely believed that the two men, and certainly Lieutenant Cranfield, had killed O'Halloran as an act of vengeance for the deaths of ten invaluable 14 Intelligence Company 'Freds', or turncoats, and the subsequent suicide of Corporal Phillips. As retaliation for this, as well as for Cranfield's illegal cross-border 'snatches', Quinn was going to assassinate Cranfield and seriously damage British morale into the bargain.

'It's clear from what Quinn says,' Lampton told Ricketts, 'that he doesn't know that O'Leary, his PIRA bookkeeper, is Cranfield's tout.'

'Which means he can't possibly know that O'Leary is setting him up to be taken out by Cranfield, instead of vice versa, and that Cranfield has deliberately used O'Halloran's murder, as well as the death of that boy in the Divis, to make Quinn go for him and give him a legal reason for ambushing him. Cranfield wants a very public hit and propaganda victory, as well as some glory for himself. He wants to be the top man.'

'Which he'll be if he succeeds.'

'Yes, if he succeeds. But if he fails, that failure will also be public and do us serious damage.'

'Shit!' Lampton exclaimed, though in a whisper. 'It goes against the grain of every SAS tenet. It's self-aggrandizement on a monumental scale. What the hell can we do?'

'Nothing,' Ricketts said. 'We can't even get out of this loft on our own. We can only get out when the Army comes back on another phoney cordon-and-search, and neither Dubois nor Cranfield will ask for that until they're good and ready.'

'Are you saying we're trapped here?' Lampton asked.

'I reckon so,' Ricketts said.

Temporary escape from the claustrophobia of the loft came through communication via the Pace Communications Landmaster III hand-held transceiver, operating in the VHF/UHF frequency range, or through the UHG band on their portable radio. Ricketts and Lampton were able to do this even when manning the surveillance equipment, as they were both equipped with Davis M135b covert microphones with standard safety-pin attachment and ear-worn receivers, positioned on the collars of their jackets, with the on/off switches taped to their wrists. One of these was tuned in to the military command network at Lisburn; the other to the surveillance network, including the two OPs in Armagh.

It was also to military HQ in Lisburn, where

Captain Dubois and Lieutenant Cranfield were based for the duration of this surveillance, and to the two OPs in south Armagh that details of Quinn's plans and movements, as picked up by the surveillance equipment, were relayed by Lampton or Ricketts in short-burst transmissions. As Quinn had suddenly taken to commuting almost daily between Belfast and his cottage in south Armagh, for meetings with other PIRA members, when such plans and movements were discussed, the two OPS in south Armagh were sending similar information back to Lisburn. Based on the information received, Cranfield was going to pick his time for taking out Quinn's PIRA ASU.

'What he wants,' Lampton said, 'is to ambush Quinn when he and his mates are embarked on some illegal PIRA activity. That's what all this surveillance is for. Also, you can bet that when the sum total of our intelligence gathering is regurgitated in edited form by 14 Intelligence Company, under the supervision of Cranfield's nervous friend, Captain Dubois, what you'll have is a report indicating that Quinn was plotting to assassinate Cranfield, but not saying exactly why. More likely it'll imply that it's because Cranfield is a supremely efficient SAS officer, deemed as a threat to the IRA in general and PIRA in particular. This will only enhance Cranfield's reputation and give him an excuse to go for Quinn. I bet Cranfield is good at chess.'

'Diabolical,' Ricketts said. 'But if he fails, he's going to do the SAS enormous harm.' He squinted through the viewfinder of the Minimodulux image intensifier on the Nikon and saw only the drawn curtains and closed front door of Michael Quinn's house. 'Let's face it, the SAS haven't exactly done themselves proud here so far. First, two troopers try to rob a bank in Londonderry and get six months for their troubles. Then we get a reputation as a bunch of killers as bad as the Black and Tans. Now we're arriving in force with a lot of men experienced in jungle or desert warfare, but with no Combat Training experience and no knowledge of the law when it comes to fighting a war on British territory. Given all this, it won't take too much to damage our reputation further – and what Cranfield's doing could do just that.'

'If you can't beat 'em, join 'em,' Lampton said. 'So if we can't stop Cranfield – and we can't – then let's make sure he doesn't fail and leave Hereford with egg on its face.'

'Mmmmm,' Ricketts murmured.

For the next couple of days he tried to concentrate on the job in hand, studying the street in general and Quinn's house in particular, by day and by night, with the aid of his hand-held thermal imager, the Minimodulux image intensifier and, most importantly, the fibre-optic probe camera inserted in the wall of the adjoining house and transmitting back to the laser system in the loft. Thus able to see and hear Quinn and his friends at all times, Ricketts and the others were given a comprehensive picture of exactly what they were doing and how they lived.

It was always difficult to know if an IRA or PIRA member truly believed in the cause or was in it for some other motive. While many had suffered either personally or indirectly at the hands of the British in the past and therefore had genuine motives for fighting them, it was an unfortunate truth that many others simply thrived on the Troubles and had good reason to ensure that they continued. Given the nature of the conflict, it was also an unfortunate truth that dedication and exploitation often tended to become muddled until even the sincere individual had forgotten his original motives and surrendered to the corruption inherent in the situation.

Though the Troubles had sprung out of genuine grievances, the hard fact of the matter was that much of Belfast was now ruled by graft, blackmail and purely mercenary violence, with protection rackets in abundance and gangs competing to rule their own patch, rewarding those who pleased them, punishing those who did not, and in general using the Troubles as a route to personal power. In this unsavoury stew, therefore, it was difficult to tell if a man was a genuine 'freedom fighter' or just another crook.

That difficulty presented itself when Ricketts and the others observed Quinn. Certainly, it was evident that he ruled his own street, was given due respect from his neighbours, and received a constant stream of visitors to his modest terraced house. Most of the visitors were men, either seasoned PIRA co-workers or adolescent dickers who came to Quinn for discussion or instruction. It was clear from the conversations that weapons were being handed over and taken back, usually accompanied by murmurs about 'single shot', 'both knees', 'six-pack', 'house call', 'post office' or 'bookie's', suggesting a combination of PIRA punishments, door-stop assassinations and armed robberies of local establishments. It also appeared, from the conversations, that Quinn doled out the weapons and that they had to be returned when the job was done.

Money also changed hands. It was usually brought in by the older men, who would hand it over while mentioning the names of various pubs, fish-and-chip shops, general stores or betting shops, occasionally saying things like: 'We fire-bombed some sense into the stupid git and now he's only too willin'.'

O'Leary, the tout below, had visited Quinn's house once since getting out of Castlereagh, attending a PIRA meeting. During a conversation about 'funds' and 'more money for weapons', the 'books' were mentioned by Quinn and O'Leary said he would have them ready soon. When Lampton observed that O'Leary sounded nervous, Taff Burgess responded: 'I can understand that – what with us being up in his loft and all. How would *you* feel?'

'I guess you're right,' Lampton said.

At least once each day, Quinn drove with some of the others to his house in Armagh. From information picked up by the OPs overlooking the house, it appeared that he was there to receive daily supplies of weapons being brought in from across the border, probably in hidden compartments in the vehicles.

'He can't be using his country place as an ammunition dump,' Lampton said to Ricketts. 'That would be too dangerous.'

'No,' Ricketts replied. 'Not an ammunition dump. Obviously he's preparing for some forth-coming outrage – something pretty big. Let's just pray that we find out about it in time to prevent it.'

'He keeps mentioning Cranfield,' Lampton recalled.

'That's what worries me,' Ricketts said.

Resting in the corner beside the sleeping Taff Burgess, Gumboot suddenly perked up to say: 'This tout down below us. The one letting us use his loft. Being a tout is one thing – you run the risk of kneecapping – but letting Brits into your loft is something else again. In fact, it's practically suicidal. What would make O'Leary do it for Cranfield?'

Lampton shook his head. 'I don't know.'

'It must be something pretty heavy,' Gumboot said, 'for O'Leary to risk that.'

'Right,' Ricketts said.

'Why do men become touts?'

'Disillusionment,' Lampton suggested. 'Moral revulsion. Money, of course.'

'Exactly,' Gumboot said. 'Money. Isn't O'Leary a PIRA bookkeeper?'

'We picked that up from Quinn,' Ricketts said.

'So maybe he needed money really bad.'

'He was fiddling the books?'

'Right. So he somehow gets involved with 14 Intelligence Company and ends up with Cranfield. I say the man's being paid.'

'So, what's your point?'

'If this guy's fiddled PIRA books and is getting Cranfield to bail him out, I'd say that Cranfield's treading tricky water and risking O'Leary's life. Those bastards across the road, if they ever find out we've been here, they're gonna bury O'Leary. That's not the SAS way, folks.'

'It's Lieutenant Cranfield's way,' Lampton said.

'He's certainly let O'Leary go out on a limb,' Ricketts said. 'Out just about as far as you can go without falling off.'

'He must've had something on him,' Gumboot said.

'Blackmail?' Lampton asked.

'What else?' Gumboot replied.

As one day passed into the next and the surveillance intelligence built up, it became clear from what Quinn said, both in Belfast and in Armagh, that he thought of Cranfield as the prime threat to PIRA and was intending to take him out. Equally clear to Ricketts was that Cranfield was virtually using himself as bait to bring Quinn's gang out into the open, where he could legally, and more publicly, put an end to them. Even more disturbing was the fact that he appeared to be using dubious means of accomplishing his mission and was doing so without consulting his superiors in the intelligence community, let alone those in Hereford. It was this that made him dangerous.

Nevertheless, regardless of their personal feelings, Ricketts and Lampton, with the able assistance of Gumboot and Taff, continued to keep watch on the house across the road and transmit what they found to Lisburn and the OPs in Armagh. Which is how they discovered that something had gone wrong with the OP covering the road to Dublin.

They knew that something had happened because communications to that OP were suddenly cut. Before they could make enquiries, they received a communication from Cranfield in Lisburn, informing them that the OP had been dismantled, for reasons which would be explained later. They were, however, to keep in touch with the OP overlooking the A1 running between Belfast and Quinn's cottage.

When Lampton asked how long they had to remain in the loft, Cranfield's message was terse: 'Sit tight.'

Given that they could not leave the loft unaided, they had no choice but to do as they were told.

Later that day, however, when listening to a conversation between Quinn and his murder squad, they heard the full story of the terminated OP.

They were still in a state of shock, trying to take it in, when they heard Quinn telling his men that they were going to attack, and take out, the other OP.

Lampton contacted Lisburn.

11

'Arrested!' Dubois practically screamed. 'Your damned troopers have actually been arrested! Explain *that* to me, Cranfield!'

Cranfield was standing by the window in an office in Army HQ Lisburn, gazing down on the courtyard surrounded by high brick walls and filled with Saracens, armoured pigs, paddy-wagons, and uniformed British soldiers and paratroopers and RUC officers in flak jackets. It looked like a fortress. Sighing, Cranfield turned back to Dubois.

'You know the score,' he said blandly. 'From time to time, on an unmarked border, soldiers *do* stray into the south.'

'Not *my* soldiers!' Dubois snapped.

'They have done so in the past and you know it, so let's not be so high and mighty about it.'

Dubois lit a cigarette and exhaled a cloud of smoke. 'All right,' he said. 'I'll try to avoid nitpicking, but this incident is rapidly inflating into a diplomatic incident, so tell me exactly what happened and we'll go on from there.'

Cranfield walked to a chair, was about to sit down, changed his mind and went back to the window, though this time standing with his back to it, in order to face the agitated Dubois. 'It happened two days ago,' he said, 'just before midnight on the fifth.' He shrugged. 'I can only put it down to their lack of experience.'

'Just tell me,' Dubois said.

'It was the men in the OP overlooking the road that runs past Quinn's cottage to Dublin. They had observed – as had the other OP overlooking the road to Belfast – that Quinn was visiting the place regularly to receive daily supplies of arms and ammunition brought in from the Free State.'

'How did they know what the supplies were?'

'Through Quinn's conversations with the suppliers. Both OPs were equipped with STG laser surveillance systems and Quinn's cottage is bugged with a fibre-optic probe camera that still transmits back to the remaining OP.'

'Go on.'

Cranfield took a deep breath, then released it again, which was the nearest he had ever come to publicly displaying nervousness. 'After observing this for three or four days, Sergeant Manners, in charge of the OP, became convinced that he was observing major PIRA suppliers and that if he followed them back to where they had come from, he would find their HQ. As the suppliers arrived about the same time every day, Manners called up a Q car from Bessbrook . . .'

'Christ!' Dubois exclaimed involuntarily.

'. . . then, leaving two of his men in the OP, but accompanied by one of his troopers, only recently badged, he went down to where the Q car was parked – out of sight of Quinn's place but with a clear view of it – and waited until that day's supply of arms had been delivered. When the suppliers drove off again, Manners ordered the driver of the Q car to follow them.'

Dubois sucked on his cigarette, screwed up his eyes and blew out a cloud of smoke like a man who can't believe what he is hearing. 'Every rule in the book broken,' he said. 'An absolute cowboy!'

Cranfield nodded. 'Anyway, Manners followed the PIRA suppliers towards Louth until the driver, navigating with the aid of a torch-lit map, took a wrong turning near Carlingford Lough. Please bear in mind that he'd been sent to Northern Ireland direct from Oman, with no chance to retrain for the very different environment of the Irish border with its confusing web of often unmarked country lanes.'

'So he got lost,' Dubois said in a flat voice.

'Yes . . . and the Q car was stopped at a police roadblock near Cornamucklagh, only 600 yards south of the border.'

Dubois leaned across the desk to cover his face with his hands. He had just inhaled again and the smoke from his cigarette drifted out from between his pursed lips.

'Go on,' he said again, more softly this time.

'Questioned by the Gardai, the SAS men claimed they were on a reconnaissance mission and had made a map-reading error. This was greeted with scepticism, and in spite of appeals to let the patrol return north, the Gardai insisted on taking advice from Dundalk. Then matters took a turn for the worse.'

'What could be worse?' Dubois asked pointedly, still cupping his face with his hands.

'When Sergeant Manners and his trooper still hadn't returned to the OP by first light, the other sergeant in the OP, also fresh from Oman, called up another Q car from Bessbrook and, with the remaining trooper, left the OP and went off to find the two missing men.'

'This is horrendous,' Dubois said, looking up and gazing fixedly beyond Cranfield to the window, clearly wishing to take wing and fly away.

'Taking the same route as Manners,' Cranfield continued, 'the second two arrived at the same Gardai checkpoint about 8 a.m. Naturally they were detained as well.'

'Unbelievable!' Dubois exclaimed bitterly.

'Weapons taken from the four men included Sterling sub-machine-guns with silencers, pump-action shotguns and the standard-issue Browning High Power. The Gardai were suitably impressed and ushered all four soldiers into the police office for further questioning. Reportedly, when the SAS men realized they had stumbled across the border and were in the Republic, they all burst out laughing.'

'Did they indeed?' Dubois stubbed his cigarette out with suppressed fury, then looked up at Cranfield. 'Unfortunately, the Irish aren't so amused. In previous cases of accidental border crossings the soldiers were reprimanded and sent back. However, as a man was recently kidnapped in that area, then brought to this side of the border and murdered, the Gardai insisted that your men be held overnight and a forensic test carried out on their weapons, to ascertain if any of them might have been used for that murder.' Pleased to see Cranfield shocked at last, Dubois nodded and said: 'Yes, Cranfield, I know what's going on. I didn't know what your men were doing in the Republic, but I know what's happening now and why your men were held overnight with the personal permission of no less than the Foreign Minister himself.'

Cranfield took a seat, clearly shaken but determined to stay calm. 'So what were the results?'

'Lucky for you, the tests proved negative. Nevertheless, though your men will be released on bail and sent back to Hereford, the Irish are calling for them to be returned eventually for trial. Naturally the British are furious about this, viewing it as a politically motivated act by the Irish government.

They've been compelled, however, to agree to send the men back when a trial can be arranged, which should be a few months from now. In the meantime, please see to it that your men, when returned to Bessbrook, are put on the first plane back to RAF Lyneham.'

'Yes, Captain,' Cranfield said.

'I take it that the OP constructed by those fools has been demolished.'

'Yes, Captain.'

'And the other one? The one overlooking the road to Belfast?'

'It's still there, manned by four good men.'

'You may need them,' Dubois said. 'We've just received a flurry of short-burst transmissions from the OP in the Falls. They were informed by the OP overlooking the Belfast road about the arms deliveries to Quinn's house. Then, listening in to Quinn's conversations, they discovered that he had found out from a source in Dublin that the SAS troops captured by the Gardai had come from an OP overlooking his place in Armagh. Quinn put that area under observation just before one of our Gazelles dropped a team to demolish it. Alerted by this, he had the area checked further and found the second OP – the one overlooking the road to Belfast.'

'Damn!' Cranfield exclaimed in frustration. 'What's he planning to do?'

'As he can't be seen to be involved himself, he

intends sending two PIRA ASUs to Armagh tomorrow – one to attack and take out the remaining OP, the other to spirit the arms out of his country place before we investigate the deaths of our OP team and, subsequently, search that same house. Meanwhile, Quinn himself will remain in the Falls, keeping his hands clean and with lots of witnesses to confirm where he was at the time of the incident.'

'My God,' Cranfield said softly, looking pleased instead of shocked. 'This is just what we need!'

Dubois had been expecting the reaction, but it still shocked him slightly. 'It's just what *you* need,' he emphasized, 'and unfortunately, whether or not I like it, I'll have to go along with it.'

'We have a legitimate excuse – self-defence. That then gives us the excuse to do a cordon-and-search of the whole area, thus finding the cache in Quinn's cottage, which in turn lets us take him in eventually and plant him in Long Kesh. It's perfect!'

'Nothing's perfect,' Dubois said, 'and I still have my doubts, but clearly we can't miss this opportunity. Can your four men handle it?'

'Yes. They took a GPMG with them and are otherwise well armed. If they're warned, they'll be ready.'

'Quinn's men are gathering at his Belfast house tomorrow at noon and leaving in three separate cars at separate times. According to the surveillance report from the OP facing his house, they'll leave Belfast empty-handed and congregate in Quinn's place in Armagh. There, while four of them pack the armaments into a van to take them elsewhere, the other four will pick the weapons they need and then engage in what they imagine will be a surprise attack on the OP. The use of an RPG 7 rocket launcher was mentioned, so your men had better be prepared to leave the OP and set up an ambush.'

'Right,' Cranfield said. He stood up and walked to the door, preparing to take his leave.

'You have a lot to make amends for,' Dubois said.

'I will,' Cranfield replied. Then, smiling brightly, already shucking off his guilt, he opened the door and hurried out, keen to get things organized.

12

It was Danny who first saw the light of the helicopter, hovering like a UFO in the dark sky just before dawn.

On watch at the viewing hole shaped out of the hedgerow and camouflaged in hessian, scanning the area around Quinn's cottage with a pair of binoculars instead of the tripod-mounted thermal imager, Danny was really just trying to distract himself until it was time to waken Martin and let him take over the watch.

Being a working-class lad from the Midlands, reticent at the best of times, unwilling to put himself forward, Danny wasn't sure that he liked Martin, who appeared to have the natural confidence of someone well educated and brought up in the security of the middle class.

In fact, Danny thought Martin was a younger version of Lieutenant Cranfield, who was, in Danny's view, a 'big timer' of the kind not normally encouraged by the SAS.

No, Danny preferred Sergeant 'Dead-eye Dick'

Parker, who, strangely enough, seemed to fill other men with dread. That, Danny reasoned, was because Dead-eye was so quiet and tended to keep to himself. Danny didn't mind that. Indeed, he thought it was a virtue. He certainly preferred it to the cockiness of men like Cranfield and Renshaw.

Of course the latter had been badged at the same time as Danny, undergoing the same Selection and Training course and, Danny had to admit, emerging from the ordeal with flying colours. Yet although Danny respected him for this, he still didn't feel comfortable with him – probably because he was intimidated by middle-class self-assurance, particularly in people his own age.

He didn't mind it so much in Cranfield, who was older and, as an officer, not so close to him.

Jock McGregor was OK. A bit of a laugh, in fact. Along with Ricketts and Dead-eye, he had been one of the SAS troopers who, four years earlier, had scaled the mighty Jebel Dhofar in Oman to flush the fierce *Adoo* fighters from the summit. Once a 'secret' war, now a legendary SAS achievement, the Dhofar campaign was exactly the kind of adventure that Danny desperately wanted to have.

Belfast, though gaining him valuable experience, was not quite so exotic. On the other hand, it had at least put him in the company of the notorious Dead-eye. The latter had also been in Oman and, according to Jock and Ricketts, was one of the best marksmen in the Regiment, as well as being deadly with his knife. Also, according to gossip, he had been a normal, fairly sociable young man until he went into the Telok Anson swamp in the Malayan jungle to fight the fierce guerrillas of Ah Hoi, nicknamed the 'Baby Killers'. Dead-eye never discussed what happened in that swamp, but he had emerged from it changed for all time. Now, he was a steely-eyed, introverted, highly efficient soldier who even made many of his fellow SAS men nervous.

Danny, who had wanted to be a soldier since he was a child, admired Dead-eye for that and was dying to know just what kind of experience had changed him so dramatically. In fact, it was Danny's belief that of all the people in the Squadron, Dead-eye was the only one with the 'secret' of how to be a great soldier – which is what he wanted to be.

Danny was thinking such thoughts when he saw a light hovering in the dark sky, like a flying saucer, then gradually taking the shape of a helicopter. At first thinking it was on a resup mission to one of the overt OPs, he soon realized that it was actually passing over the distant hills and coming straight towards him. When the sound of it reached him, growing louder by the second, he glanced back over his shoulder and saw that Dead-eye was already awake and sitting up to find out what was happening.

'Is that a chopper?' Dead-eye asked as Jock and Martin also woke up, rubbing sleepy eyes.

'Yes,' Danny said. 'And it seems to be coming straight at us.'

Dead-eye scrambled across the OP to glance out of the viewing hole. By that time the chopper was identifiable as a Gazelle flying from the direction of Bessbrook and dropping down towards the OP.

'We're supposed to be on a *secret* mission,' Danny said, 'so what are *they* doing here?'

Dead-eye didn't reply. Instead, he watched the chopper descending. It came down towards the OP, hovered above it for a moment, then glided south and landed behind it, just far enough away for its spinning rotors not to sweep the loose grass and gorse off the camouflaged hessian. Dead-eye grabbed a Colt Commando – he never moved without a weapon – and crawled out of the OP. Automatically picking up his M16, Danny followed him.

'We'll stay here,' Jock shouted after him, 'and keep our eye on the target!'

'You do that,' Danny whispered.

As he crawled out of the OP he saw Lieutenant Cranfield hurrying away from the Gazelle, crouched low against the wind generated by the rotors. Wearing DPMs and a beret with badge, he had a Browning High Power holstered on his hip. Danny climbed to his feet as Cranfield straightened up and approached the watchful Dead-eye. He hurried to stand beside his hero and hear what was said.

'Morning, Sergeant,' Cranfield said. Dead-eye just nodded. The spinning rotors of the Gazelle went into neutral, thus reducing the noise considerably and letting the men hear each other speak. 'How are things up here?'

'Fine,' Dead-eye said. 'No problems. Nothing much happening either way.'

'You heard about the other OP team, I gather?'

Dead-eye nodded. 'Fucking twats.'

'Right,' Cranfield said. 'The OP's been demolished and the men are being flown back to Hereford. The Irish, however, are insisting that they be returned later to Northern Ireland to be put on trial. Downing Street has agreed.'

'A show trial.'

'Yes. Not that they don't deserve it. I trust that you men will show more sense.'

Danny glimpsed a flash of anger in Dead-eye, but his voice remained flat. 'What are you doing here, Lieutenant? This is supposed to be a *covert* OP.'

'Your cover's been blown, Sergeant. Someone in Dublin traced that other OP team back to here and Quinn had the area thoroughly searched. Now Quinn knows that this second OP is here and he intends taking it out.'

'When?'

'Today. Two four-man ASUs will soon be on their way here from the Falls – one to take out the OP, leaving no one alive; the other to remove the weapons and ammunition from

Quinn's place, leaving him looking like Mister Clean.'

'You picked that up from the OP in the Falls?'

'Yes.'

'That was useful.'

'Lampton's team is doing a good job.'

'So what do we do about the ASUs? Are we staying or leaving?'

'You're staying. They're expecting to take you by surprise, but instead you're going to be waiting for them to reverse expectations.'

'An ambush.'

'Correct. They're coming with an RPG 7 rocket launcher, so you have to take them out before they can fire a rocket at the OP. If you manage to do it before Quinn's place is cleared, you can then go down and take out the others.'

'You don't want them captured?'

'I didn't say that. I'm merely saying that I want you to inflict as much damage as possible within the strict letter of the law. It's legitimate self-defence.'

Dead-eye gazed steadily at Cranfield in a silence that seemed to last a long time. Eventually, when the officer didn't flinch, he asked: 'What if we succeed?'

'You call Bessbrook with the results of the action. We'll then lift you out and clean up the damage.'

'What about Quinn, all cosy in Belfast?'

'When we catch the others trying to clear out his cottage – which I expect you to do – we can haul him into Crumlin Road jail as the start of his legal journey to Long Kesh. There we'll slam the door on him.'

'When are the ASUs expected to get here?'

'About noon.'

'That gives us plenty of time. Have you come to help out?'

'I'd love to, but I can't,' Cranfield said. 'Unfortunately, this action has to look like self-defence, not something planned, so I can't be seen to be part of it – and this little visit, incidentally, never happened.'

'What's the story?'

'Having had Quinn's cottage under surveillance for some time, you'd seen his men bringing in weapons, ammunition and explosives. You were deciding what to do about it when an ASU hit squad almost took you by surprise. Luckily, you saw them coming and were able to hit them before they hit you. Then you saw another bunch removing the weapons from the cottage, so you went after them as well, to stop them escaping. That's the story. Stick to it.'

'Will do,' Dead-eye said.

'Good luck, Sergeant.'

'Thanks.'

Cranfield returned to the Gazelle and climbed back in. The rotors slipped out of neutral, started spinning faster, soon whipping up a minor storm, then lifted the chopper up off the hill. Dead-eye watched it flying off towards Bessbrook, beyond lush hills now visible in morning light, then he glanced flatly at Danny and nodded towards the OP.

Danny went in first, with Dead-eye following him. Jock was having a breakfast of cheese and biscuits washed down with water. Martin was adjusting the bulky, tripod-mounted, Thorn EMI thermal imager at the viewing hole, but he turned around to face them when they entered.

'Who was it?' Jock asked.

'Lieutenant Cranfield,' Dead-eye replied.

'What the fuck did *he* want?' Jock asked, with no great respect.

Dead-eye filled him in on the situation as explained by Lieutenant Cranfield. 'The ASUs should be here about noon,' he summarized, 'and we have to be ready.'

'So what's the strategy, boss?' Martin asked, sounding excited.

Dead-eye stared steadily at him, then turned slightly aside, speaking mainly to Jock. 'They have an RPG 7 rocket launcher, so my bet is they'll stop part of the way up the hill to lob one into the OP, thinking we're in it. Given the elevation requirements of the RPG 7, they'll have to fire it from near the bottom of the hill, not much higher than the lower slopes, so that's where we'll locate – to take them out before they can fire the missile.'

'Sounds good,' Jock said.

'There's a hedgerow running down the side of the hill, about fifty yards west of the OP. Three of us will dig in there, near to where it levels out, and wait for the bastards to arrive. The fourth man will remain here on the GPMG to give us cover when the fire-fight commences.'

'If we're down that low,' Jock reminded him, 'we'll be close to the road, which puts us within range of the fire-power of the ASU team clearing out Quinn's place.'

'Exactly,' Dead-eye said. 'Which gives us a legitimate excuse to attack them as well and get our hands on the incriminating evidence – the weapons, ammo and explosives from Quinn's cottage.'

'One of Cranfield's little dodges.'

'Pretty damned good,' Martin said. 'He's a hell of an officer, Lieutenant Cranfield. He knows just what he's doing.'

'I'll *bet* he does,' Jock said. 'So who stays in the OP?'

'You,' Dead-eye told him. 'Apart from me, you're the most experienced, so you shouldn't need supervision. I trust you to use your initiative and not make mistakes.'

'Such as shooting us instead of the ASU team,' Martin said with a wide grin.

'If I shoot you,' Jock said, 'it'll be intentional. I don't make mistakes.'

'You two,' Dead-eye said to Martin and Danny, 'will come with me and do what I tell you. We'll need short-handled pickaxes and spades for the scrapes. Attach the M203 grenade launchers to your M16s. At my signal, you'll lay two grenades down on the ASU. When they explode, Jock'll take that as the signal to open up with the GPMG. What damage not inflicted by Jock, will be inflicted by us. OK, let's get going.'

'They're not coming until noon,' Martin reminded him.

'You've got something better to do up here, Trooper?' Dead-eye asked.

'No, boss.'

'Then let's get the fuck down that hill and make sure we're ready. They might get here *before* noon.'

'Yes, boss!' Martin snapped.

'Whatever way it goes,' Jock said, 'this OP is finished, so take that thermal imager away and let me put the machine-gun in its place.'

'Right,' Martin said. 'But I'll leave the Nikon with the image intensifier so that you can take photos when they arrive. They'll be helpful as evidence.'

Jock glanced at Dead-eye who simply nodded, acknowledging that Martin, though cocky, was right.

'Aye,' Jock said, 'you do that.'

Dead-eye and Danny checked their weapons, ensured that they had a plentiful supply of 30-round magazines, then clipped short-handled spades and pickaxes to their belts. As they were doing so,

Jock set up the tripod for the GPMG. Meanwhile, Martin unscrewed the bulky thermal imager from its tripod, then removed it and the tripod from in front of the viewing hole. Martin placed the thermal imager back in its canvas carrier while Jock set the GPMG up on its tripod, with the barrel poking out through the viewing hole, angled down the hill, beside the Nikon with the image intensifier, also mounted on a tripod at the viewing hole. As Jock was feeding the ammunition belt into the GPMG, which normally required a two-man team, Dead-eye slid a spade and a pickaxe towards Martin, saying: 'Here, clip these to your belt and take as many magazines as you can reasonably carry. Plus fragmentation and buckshot grenades for the M203s. Let's give them a sore arse.'

Martin grinned and did as he was told.

'Are you OK, Jock?' Dead-eye asked.

Jock, now sitting on a wooden box behind the GPMG, stuck his thumb up in the air. 'Straight line-of-sight between here and the cottage. Can't miss, boss.'

'You fire when the grenades go off,' Dead-eye reminded him. 'One belt's all you need.'

'No sweat,' Jock said.

'OK,' Dead-eye said to the others. 'Let's get the fuck down that hill. See you later, Jock.'

'Right, boss,' Jock said.

Holding his 5.56mm Colt Commando in the Belfast Cradle, Dead-eye crawled out, followed by

Martin and Danny. Once outside, in the grey light of morning, they straightened up and headed down the hill at a half crouch, zigzagging automatically over the boulder-strewn grass and turf, heading obliquely towards the tall fuchsia hedges that bordered the western side of the field, beyond which was an undulating landscape of green fields and trees. When they had reached the fuchsia hedges, Dead-eye led them further down until they were about fifty metres from the fence separating the hill from the road running across the front of Quinn's cottage – one way to Belfast, the other to Dublin.

'Our patch,' Dead-eye said.

Wearing DPM clothing, and with their weapons wrapped in tape of a similar colouring, they blended into the hedges even before digging out their scrapes. Nevertheless, using their short-handled pickaxes and spades, they made themselves shallow scrapes that extended into the foliage, letting it fall back over them when they crawled in and lay on their bellies. Though not comfortable, they were practically invisible and ready to fire.

Glancing to his right, downhill, Danny could see the road beyond the fence and, behind that, Quinn's cottage. It was a nondescript building, with brick walls and slate roof, two storeys high, but set well back from the road, surrounded by high, rolling fields, with no other houses in sight. A modest but very pleasant country retreat, it was now a warehouse packed with weapons, ammunition and explosives.

Fire a grenade in there, Danny thought, *and the whole place will go up in flames. That's not a house; it's an arsenal.*

Lying belly down in his shallow scrape, half buried in the foliage, cradling his M16 with an M203 grenade launcher attached, with Dead-eye on one side of him and Martin Renshaw on the other, Danny suddenly realized that his Selection and Training were over and that this was the real thing.

He had been in the Army for two years, 3rd Battalion, Light Infantry, but this was the first time he'd been involved in an actual conflict, let alone being out of England. His couple of days in Belfast, doing the 'tour' with Sergeant Hampton of 14 Intelligence Company, had presented him with a graphic picture of a city at war with itself. Yet it had not led to actual engagement with the enemy. Now all that was about to change and he wondered how he would deal with it when push came to shove.

You'll be OK, he told himself.

Danny had wanted to be a special kind of soldier since his schooldays – thinking first about the French Foreign Legion, then about becoming a mercenary, but eventually accepting that it had to be legitimate and so deciding on joining the army, in order to serve his requisite two years and then apply for the SAS. Having decided, he had done it and never regretted it, feeling that he was born to be a soldier. Now here he was, about to fire his first shots in anger, thankfully with Dead-eye by his side. That made him feel good.

After an hour or so of waiting, hearing nothing but the birdsong and the occasional car passing on the road below, Danny had an almost uncontrollable urge to break the silence by asking Dead-eye about the Telok Anson swamp. Unfortunately, though he had managed to screw up the courage, he was too far away to do it without shouting, which he knew would anger the experienced sergeant.

Dead-eye had placed them about fifteen metres apart, with Martin the highest up, Dead-eye closest to the road, therefore to Quinn's cottage, and Danny in the middle. This would give them a triangular field of fire homing in on where Dead-eye had calculated the ASU would be compelled to set up the RPG 7 for the required elevation. Clearly, he knew what he was doing, though it did prevent them from passing the time with conversation. Not that Dead-eye ever talked much anyway.

Frustrated, Danny contented himself by studying the scenery – the tree-lined, bright green, alluvial fields; sunlight glinting off a stretch of sea, glimpsed beyond the distant hills; birds winging through a jigsaw of blue sky and patchy clouds – and by dwelling on how different it was from the bleak, terraced streets of Kingswinford, where he grew up. It was hard to imagine, when you looked at this scenery, that Belfast lay just beyond the hills and its streets were even worse than those in Kingswinford – worse to look at and infinitely more dangerous to live in. It was hard to imagine what was happening here, with the British fighting a mean war on British soil. Of course, the Irish didn't think it was British soil – which explained the war.

Danny was almost lost in thoughts of this kind when a red Ford came in sight, from the direction of Belfast, and pulled into a lay-by just around a slow bend in the road. Although he could see the car clearly from his vantage point halfway up the hill, Danny realized that it would be out of sight of the OP. Knowing that this must have been deliberate, he instinctively tensed, preparing himself for action.

Three men got out of the car, leaving the driver behind the wheel, presumably to do the talking should an Army or RUC patrol come along. The men were wearing normal civilian clothing: corduroy trousers or denims, jackets and open-necked shirts. One of them lay on his belly, groped under the car, and eventually withdrew a long object wrapped in some kind of covering – the RPG 7, Danny surmised. Another leaned back into the rear of the vehicle, as if groping around beneath the seats, and eventually withdrew two more long parcels – probably wrapped rifles or sub-machine-guns. The third man, meanwhile, was leaning into the rear door at the other side.

Eventually he straightened up, holding a canvas bag, which Danny assumed was filled with magazines for the weapons.

After conversing briefly with the driver, the man holding the wrapped RPG 7 led the other two through a gateway in the high fuchsia hedges and wooden fence bordering the road, into the field at a location approximately forty-five degrees east of the line-of-sight of the OP. The men then made their way alongside the road, but were shielded from it by the high hedge. They were also hidden from the OP by an abrupt dip in the ground where the field ran down steeply before levelling out near the fence.

They were able to clamber a good twenty metres up that steep, lower stretch of the hill while remaining out of view of the OP and without being seen by the few cars passing by. When eventually they chose the spot from which to launch their attack, they were just below Dead-eye, obliquely to the right of Martin and Danny.

Hidden in the hedge, Danny set the M203 grenade launcher to fire, judged the angle of elevation required, then held the M16 steady.

The red Ford remained where it was – parked just around the bend in the road, out of sight of the OP.

The man with the wrapped RPG 7 looked at his watch, then said something to the other two, who immediately began unwrapping the parcels.

The large parcel was, indeed, a wrapped RPG 7

rocket launcher and the other two were Russian 7.62mm AK-47 automatic rifles, beloved of terrorists everywhere and instantly recognizable, even from this distance, because of the unusually curved 30-round box magazine.

When the weapons were unwrapped, the man with the canvas bag opened it and started handing out ammunition, including magazines for the AK-47s and a 2.25kg missile for the RPG 7.

Danny glanced sideways and saw Dead-eye's hand thrusting out of the hedge, about to give the signal to fire.

The man with the RPG 7 checked his watch again, then glanced back over his shoulder, down the hill and across the road to Quinn's cottage. Shaking his head from side to side, as if exasperated, he loaded the 2.25kg missile into the launcher, then glanced back over his shoulder again.

A grey removal truck came along the road from the direction of the nearby border, and pulled into the driveway. Four men got out, glanced up the hill in the general direction of the covert OP, and waved.

Obviously knowing that his comrades would be seen by the OP, the man knelt in the firing position and aimed the RPG 7.

Still looking sideways, Danny saw Dead-eye drop his hand, signalling, 'Open fire.' Leaning forward into the stock of his M16, Danny fired the M213 grenade launcher.

His head was ringing from the noise, his body jolting from the backblast, as the two grenades — one fired by Martin, located higher up the hill — exploded at the same time on either side of the three men, with soil and buckshot spewing up and outwards through boiling columns of black smoke.

Even as the smoke was still obscuring the men, the shocking roar of the GPMG firing from the OP joined the harsh chatter of the M16s, as well as Dead-eye's Colt Commando.

Danny had switched to the M16 automatically, hardly aware that he had done so, and was firing rapidly repeated three-round bursts into the swirling smoke from the buckshot grenades.

One of the men was already down, bowled sideways by the blast. The other two were dancing wildly in a convulsion of spitting earth created by the combined fire-power of the GPMG and three M16 assault rifles. Taken by surprise, and confused as to where the firing was actually coming from, the remaining two didn't even have time to fire their weapons before they were cut to shreds and collapsed.

As the two men fell, the red Ford screeched into life, reversed out of the lay-by, and raced back around the bend, returning to Belfast.

At the same time, the men in the cottage, seeing what had happened, raced across the driveway to get back into the removal van.

As Jock's GPMG trailed off into silence, Dead-eye leapt out of the hedge and raced across the field, his Colt Commando in one hand, a Landmaster III transceiver in the other. As he knelt down to examine the bloody ASU team, speaking into the transceiver at the same time, the removal van lumbered out of Quinn's driveway. One of the men, however, obviously senseless with anger, bellowed a string of abuse in a broad Ulster accent, then raced across the road and clambered over the fence. He dropped down the other side, took aim with his pistol, and fired at Dead-eye.

Stepping out from the hedge, Danny adopted the kneeling position, took aim with his M16 and fired a couple of three-round bursts. The man was punched backwards so hard that he smashed through the fence, falling to the ground.

'Stop that van!' Dead-eye bellowed, pointing down the hill, then speaking again into the transceiver.

Danny switched back to the M203 and loaded a grenade while running a few more yards down the hill, followed by Martin, who was holding his M16 in the Belfast Cradle. The removal van had just driven out through the gates of the cottage and was turning into the road, in the direction of the border, when Danny calculated the angle of elevation and fired a fragmentation grenade. The backblast rocked his shoulder and his head rang from the noise. Then the grenade exploded just in front of the truck, practically under the left wheel, shattering the windscreen and lifting the whole vehicle up on to two wheels. It slammed back down again, but careered across the road, bouncing over a ditch, then smashed through the fence and embedded itself deep in the hedgerow.

Martin was already racing past Danny when first one, then two of the men in the crashed van jumped down to the ground, before straightening up and firing their pistols.

Martin fired on the run and Danny fired a second later. One of the men jerked spasmodically, dropped his pistol, fell back, and shuddered wildly against the side of the van as more bullets stitched him. He was sliding to the ground, leaving a trail of blood on the side of the van, as the other man backed across the road, firing as he retreated. He had almost reached the fence of the cottage when a combined burst from Martin and Danny nearly cut him in two, then picked him up and slammed him back on to the fence, which immediately buckled under his falling body. Pouring blood from his chest and stomach, the man rocked like a see-saw for a couple of seconds, then slowly fell backwards, into the driveway. Meanwhile, Martin and Danny were racing down the hill to check the dead and the wounded.

The only wounded was the driver of the van, his eyes bloodied and blinded by shards of glass from the shattered windscreen, his forehead split open, his nose broken by impact with the steering wheel. He was unconscious, but groaning.

The other men, including the one across the road, had been torn to shreds by the high-velocity 5.56mm bullets of the M16s. Soaked in blood, with bone gleaming through gristle, they were certainly dead.

'Let's check the house,' Martin said.

Slightly shaken by the terrible wounds inflicted on the dead, but also feeling pure and bright, as if illuminated from within, Danny followed Martin along the gravel driveway to the front of Quinn's hideaway. Obviously excited, Martin smashed the lock on the door with a single burst from his M16, then led Danny inside.

The hall was filled with wooden crates containing guns and ammunition. So was the living room. Explosives of every kind were stacked up in the kitchen, and more weapons, ammunition and explosives were found in the back room.

'Some haul!' Martin said softly.

At that moment, he was buzzed on his walkie-talkie. When he had turned it on and identified himself, the voice of Dead-eye informed him that he was to remain in the cottage until Sappers — already called up by Dead-eye — arrived to remove the weapons, ammunition and explosives for transfer to Bessbrook. Danny, Dead-eye said, was to stand guard over the crashed removal van until an ambulance, also from Bessbrook, arrived to take away the dead and wounded. A REME team had also been called up to remove the crashed, badly damaged van.

'OK, boss,' Martin said. 'We've got you. Over and out.' He switched the walkie-talkie off and grinned at Danny. 'You get the stiffs and the truck,' he said, then waved his right hand, indicating the crates piled up all around him in the living room, 'and I get all this. Let's do what the man says.'

Leaving Martin in the relative warmth of the house, Danny stepped out into the biting cold, glanced uneasily at the bloody body lying face up by the fence, then crossed the road to the crashed removal van. The driver was still unconscious, but had mercifully stopped groaning and was now lying with his forehead resting on the steering wheel, which was covered in a mass of congealed blood, some of which had dripped from his blinded eyes. Since there was little he could do for him, Danny left him as he was and went around to stand guard by the side of the van, facing the road leading to Belfast.

From where he was standing, he could see that Jock had left the OP to join Dead-eye over the bodies of the three dead terrorists, in the dip near the bottom of the hill. Dead-eye had put his Landmaster III away and was talking to Jock while scanning the Belfast road, obviously impatient for the medics, REME team and Sappers to come and clean up the mess. Eventually, they did so – first the ambulance, then the REME breakdown truck and mechanics, and finally the Sappers with their own trucks. The medics removed the dead and the one wounded man, the REME truck removed the crashed van, and the Sappers transferred the weapons, ammunition and explosives from the cottage to their vehicles, then drove back to Bessbrook. When they had all gone, Danny and Martin joined Jock and Dead-eye outside the OP.

'You men did a good job,' Dead-eye said. 'I have no complaints.'

Though swelling with pride, Danny asked quietly: 'What about the man in the red Ford?'

'I gave the car's details to Bessbrook and they set up a roadblock and helicopter recce to bring him in. They've just told me they caught him.'

'What happens now?' Martin asked.

'We demolish this OP,' Dead-eye said, 'and return to Bessbrook. A chopper will lift us off at three p.m. – precisely one hour from now.'

'A hot bath and a cold beer,' Jock said. 'Back to civilization.'

'You'll be lucky,' Dead-eye said without humour.

They packed up their kit, demolished the OP and were lifted off the hill an hour later by a Gazelle. Ten minutes later they were back in Bessbrook, watching their beer being poured in the NAAFI canteen.

'Gimme, gimme!' Jock said.

13

Lieutenant Cranfield was wearing a pinstripe suit when he met Margaret Dogherty, coming off the Dublin train at Belfast Central Station. Margaret was wearing a knee-length Wallis overcoat of grey, understated elegance, with high heels emphasizing the curves of her already long legs. Her auburn hair was falling down around her face, which was pale-skinned, smooth and surprisingly delicate, except for a latent hardness, or world weariness. Though only twenty-five, she somehow looked older, though she was still an exceptionally attractive woman.

'Have you come?' she said to Cranfield, using that oddity of greeting peculiar to the Ulster Irish.

'Yes,' Cranfield replied. 'You look wonderful. Let me carry that bag.'

She handed him the travelling bag, then took his arm and let him lead her out of the busy station.

'That's a very nice pinstripe,' Margaret said. 'Sure it makes you look like some ponce from the Civil Service.' Her Ulster accent had effectively been erased by five years in London, then another three in Dublin, but she still used certain oddities of the vernacular.

'It makes me feel so respectable,' Cranfield said, 'when I'm out of uniform. Besides, I thought you might like it. Having a gentleman on your arm, instead of some rag-and-bone man like Michael O'Leary.'

Her sideways glance was one of mockery at his arrogance. 'What does that mean?'

'He said he had to visit someone in Dublin before we lifted him out. Given the danger to him the longer he remains here, I could only imagine him taking the risk for the woman he loves.'

Margaret smiled as they left the station, heading for the taxi rank by the pavement. 'He loves my body,' she said. 'He loves what it does to him.'

'He came to it pretty late, my dear, which is why he's besotted.'

'And you're not?'

'Not with that particular kind of passion. I'm a married man, after all.'

As they slipped into the back of the black taxi, which Cranfield refused to share with other passengers, as was the local custom, he realized that he hadn't been home for two months, though it seemed a lot longer than that. Back in Eaton Bishop, nothing would have changed much. His wife Maria would be pottering about in the garden, as she did nearly every day, and his three children, Julia,

Tanya and Robert, seven, six and five respectively, would be attending private school in the soothing greenery of Hereford, free of IRA snipers and Army checkpoints. It was a nice, easy life there.

'A married man having his little bit of fun,' Margaret said as the taxi pulled away from the kerb. 'Have you no conscience, Randolph?'

'Not really. I have a happy family in Hereford. Being a good father goes a long way with most married women. Maria has few complaints.'

'Does she know you play around?'

'Of course not.'

'Does she suspect?'

'I doubt it.'

'I don't know how men can face their wives and kids after being with my kind.'

'It comes with practice, my dear.'

In fact, Cranfield enjoyed going home – it had a civilizing influence on him – but he only liked it for limited periods, invariably becoming bored and restless if there too long. He was not a man for family life, let alone monogamy, though he'd always been careful to hide that side of himself from his wife. Now, as he sat beside Margaret in the black cab, aware of the heat of her soft thigh against his own, he was free of the slightest trace of guilt, at ease with himself.

'So *did* O'Leary visit you in Dublin?' he asked her.

'Yes. Sure he wanted me to marry him. Said he

was on his way to Australia – that you were fixing it up for him. Said we could begin a new life there, free of the IRA.'

'And you said?'

'No thanks. I had my own life to live, like. I told him he'd get over me in time and find someone better. When that didn't work, I reminded him that I did this for a livin' and now know nothing else. He left with tears in his eyes.'

'Does he know we put you in his path?'

'Sure he hasn't a clue.'

'We're lifting him out a week from now – all the way to Sydney via Bangkok, with a new identity and a healthy pension. Perhaps you should have said yes.'

'I'd have to be skint to consider that. Maybe in my old age.'

'A long time to go yet,' Cranfield said.

It did not, however, take long to reach the Europa Hotel. Leaving East Bridge Street, the taxi was soon passing the back of the imposing City Hall and its lovely gardens. Again, Cranfield was struck with how attractive the centre of Belfast would be were it not for the high steel fences and Army checkpoints that blocked off the main shopping precincts.

To most of the English, Belfast was a dreadful place of slums and bricked-up houses, but these were in the minority and the city was actually very appealing, with its stately Victorian architecture, the pastoral River Lagan, numerous parks and surrounding mountains, green hills and farmlands. If Belfast was sometimes not a pretty sight, it had been scarred by the very people laying claim to it.

Even as Cranfield was dwelling on this truth, the car turned off Howard Street, down Brunswick, then made a double right through Amelia and into Great Victoria Street. The Europa Hotel was almost immediately on the left, facing the pub where Cranfield had met his Protestant tout, Norman Reid.

The taxi pulled up in front of the security huts by the electronically controlled gates of the forecourt. Cranfield and Margaret climbed out. When Cranfield had paid the driver and picked up Margaret's bag, they entered the front door of the security hut. As he checked the contents of Margaret's bag, the private security guard asked her why she was bringing it into the hotel.

'I've just arrived from Dublin,' she told him, 'but me and my fiancé' – she grinned at Cranfield – 'are staying here for the afternoon. You understand, Mister?'

The security guard didn't smile. Instead, he zipped up the bag, then briskly, efficiently frisked Cranfield. A security woman did the same to Margaret, then they were waved through the inner door of the hut, out into the courtyard with its well-guarded, wire-fenced car park.

'There's nothing like this in Dublin,' Margaret

said, shaking her head in amazement. 'Belfast's a whole other world.'

'Would you like a drink first?' Cranfield asked as they entered the lobby of the hotel.

'No. I only have a couple of hours to spare. Let's have drinks in the room. Have you signed in already?'

'Yes.'

'What a bright wee boy you are!'

Cranfield collected the key, ordered a bottle of dry white wine to be sent up, waved the bellboy away, and led Margaret into the elevator, then along to their room. Once inside, he went to the window and glanced down on Great Victoria Street, with the Crown Liquor Saloon directly across the road.

An armoured pig had just stopped to let the soldiers check a parked car. If they couldn't locate the owner, or if the car was locked, they would assume there was a bomb planted in it and call the Sappers to blow it up. In the event, even as Cranfield was looking down, a harassed businessman rushed out of the Crown and started talking frantically to the soldiers, explaining why the car was parked there. Cranfield glanced left and right along the road, instinctively looking for trouble, then, feeling foolish, turned back to the room.

Margaret was sitting on the edge of the bed and kicking off her high heels.

'So what are you doing back in Belfast?' Cranfield asked.

'My mother's dyin',' she replied, 'so I've come to stay until it's all over.'

'I'm sorry to hear that.'

'You don't give a damn and neither do I. I can't stand the old cow. She's made my life miserable.'

'Still, she's dying.'

'Ach, we all go sometime.'

'You're just here until it's over?'

'Right.'

'How long do you think it'll be?'

Margaret shrugged. 'I don't know. It's the cancer. It could take days or weeks. Sure there's no way of knowin'.'

'Where do you plan staying?'

'In the family house in Conway Street, where I was born and grew up.'

'That's off the Falls, isn't it?'

'Aye. One of the places hit hardest when the Troubles began back in sixty-nine.'

'Is it near where O'Leary lives?'

'A couple of streets away.'

'You might bump into him.'

'When did you say he's leavin'?'

'A week today.'

'I'll avoid him for as long as I can. If I see him, I'll say I'm here because of my mum. That's one truth that should work, since Irishmen, if they don't respect other women, have a fearful respect for their mothers.'

The bell on the door rang. When Cranfield asked who it was, a voice said: 'Room Service.' The young man who came in was carrying a tray containing a bottle of chilled white wine and two glasses. Cranfield tipped him handsomely, then walked behind him back across the room and locked the door when he left.

He turned back to Margaret, who had taken off her coat, as well as her shoes, and was unbuttoning her dress down the front.

'Do you enjoy this?' she asked him as he removed his coat and tie, revealing the holstered Browning beneath. 'Fucking the woman that poor bastard thinks he loves?'

'I'll admit, it amuses me,' Cranfield replied.

'You think he's a poor dumb paddy. Is that it?'

'There's a lot of them about.'

'So says the high and mighty, over-educated Englishman. Here to protect the Irish from themselves.'

'With the help of the Irish, don't forget. At least the Irish like you. What a strange lot you are.'

'You don't know anything about the Irish,' Margaret told him. 'Coming over here to fight your colonial war, you see nothing but bottle-throwing Fenians, ferocious housewives in curlers and kids who've known nothing but the violence you helped to create. I was born and raised here and what I see is what you English are destroying. This is a lively, cultured city of the kind that could put most English towns to shame – but you think of it exactly as the Protestant invaders did when they sailed up the Lagan to take over – as a place filled with simple-minded bog-men who can't count without using their fingers. Well, it isn't. It's a place of imagination, which is what you pragmatic English don't understand. Fuck me, Cranfield, but don't try to fuck with me, because I won't play that game. Now take what you paid for.'

Cranfield had his way with her, enjoying it more because of her anger, feeling, as he strained up her body, that he was fighting another war. It was something he needed, the thrill of conflict, a sense of danger, and he found it in his dealings with this woman who whored for a living and, as a lucrative sideline, risked her life by seducing men in the IRA in order to set them up as patsies for British intelligence, as she had done with O'Leary.

She did it for money, but also out of vengeance, because, as she had told him, she didn't have too much time for men in general, let alone the terrorists or so-called freedom fighters on either side. She could do it, she'd told Cranfield, because she despised all such men. Thus she rendered them faceless.

When Cranfield had asked if she included him in that, she confirmed that she did. This revelation only increased his curiosity and sexual excitement.

Now, when he had finished and rolled off her sweat-slicked body, he asked what had made her hate men so much and, in particular, his own kind – those who lived and fought in the killing grounds of what had once been her home.

'If you despise men like me so much,' he said, 'why do you then betray your own? What made you turn and work for us? It can't just be the money.'

Still naked, she turned away to light a cigarette. When he passed her a glass of chilled white wine, she blew smoke in his face.

'When the Troubles first flared up in the Bogside, I was only eighteen and didn't have a clue what was going on. The Prods came stormin' down our street, throwing Molotov cocktails and swingin' wooden stakes with nails embedded in them. They smashed heads and windows, set houses on fire, and drove most of my neighbours from their homes – so I wasn't in love with them. Then the British Army arrived. It was like Armageddon. They came in to separate the Catholics from the Prods, but instead they made enemies of both. The Falls became a war zone.'

She inhaled, blew another cloud of smoke, then sipped her wine.

'I was thick as two planks,' she said. 'Hardly knew my own name. Thinkin' that some of the British soldiers were lovely, I fancied that one would fall for me and take me out of this place. I wasn't the only one, believe me. A lot of us were like that.

We'd throw stones during the day and fraternize with them at night, when they were wearin' their civvies. Of course that was my downfall.'

She rolled over and swung her legs out of the sheets, to sit on the edge of the bed. The sight of her took Cranfield's breath away, but he knew enough to keep his hands off her now.

'Once the Army settled in,' she continued, sounding faraway, 'the Catholic hard men came out of the woodwork and took over the streets. They also took over our lives, spyin' on us, demandin' protection money and punishin' those seen to go against them – with beatings, kneecappings and executions. At first it was mostly men who were victims, but soon enough they got around to the women. Men always do, don't they?'

She inhaled deeply, blew a cloud of smoke, then stubbed out her half-finished cigarette. Shuddering, she had another drink of wine, then placed the glass on her bare thigh.

'Me and my girlfriend, Peggy – she was only seventeen – were caught drinkin' with some Brits in a pub at the lower end of Grosvenor Street, in what we innocently thought was neutral territory. The two soldiers, sweet lads, were in civvies, but that only made matters worse. They were badly beaten, dragged out of the pub, then had their throats cut with a butcher's knife. I know this because me and Peggy were dragged out of the pub and forced to look at their dead, bloody bodies.

Then we were beaten up as well and sent home black and blue.'

She reached for another cigarette, changed her mind, and finished off her glass of wine instead. Cranfield silently topped up her glass and let her continue.

'Me and Peggy, God help us, were in a state of shock, but thought that at least the worst was over. Unfortunately, it wasn't. In fact, for us it was just beginning. For the next couple of days, when we dared to venture out, the men in the street would shout filthy comments and often spit at us. Naturally, when the men did it enough, the women followed suit. After a couple of days of this, we were both terrified to go out – we lived practically door-to-door – but on the fourth day the bastards came for us.'

She had another drink, almost finishing it all. As Cranfield topped her up, she lit another cigarette, inhaling deeply and exhaling as if she couldn't breathe properly. Eventually, back in control, she continued her dreadful tale.

'They dragged the two of us out of our houses at the same time. They were like one of those lynch mobs you see outside British courts when someone's raped or murdered a child – all punching, spitting, trying to tear our hair out. In the event, with regard to our hair, they were wasting their time.'

She had another drink, took a deep breath, let it out with a shuddering sigh.

'We were tied to lampposts. One of our neighbours, a woman, hacked our hair off with scissors, leaving both of us practically bald. Then a man came along with a bucket of hot tar and painted us with it – head, face, neck, arms and body, even our bare legs. When he had finished, his cronies, brave men one and all, threw bucketfuls of chicken feathers over us, until we were thoroughly tarred and feathered. They left us there, tied to the lampposts, for the passers-by to enjoy.'

'Christ!' Cranfield whispered.

'Ironically, it was a British Army patrol who released us, though they weren't sympathetic. "Fenian whores!" one of them muttered as he cut through the ropes. "You fucking deserve what you get." My mother, when she found out what had happened, said practically the same thing. So did Peggy's mother. That was what we got for bein' too young and not all that bright. It traumatized me for years.'

She stood up, drained her glass and set it back on the table, then turned to face Cranfield. 'I never forgave my mother for that. Never did, never will. Nor did I forgive those bastards who tarred and feathered me, then left me tied to that lamppost, for everyone to laugh at. When I'd recovered from my shock – and that took months, not days – I packed up and went alone to London, to make a new life for myself. I ended up, wouldn't you know, as just another Irish tart at King's Cross, doing lots for a little. Then I got my senses back, moved down to Mayfair, and learnt that being a whore for the wealthy was a lot easier, and certainly more lucrative, than spreadin' my legs for the poor. One of the people I fucked in my Mayfair flat was from British Intelligence.'

'Which gets you to me,' Cranfield said.

'Right. After getting rid of my accent – the last reminder of my roots – I moved to Dublin, did the tourist and middle-class trade, and picked up a few wee jobs for your fine friends in Whitehall. I returned to get my own back on the bastards . . . and that's why I'm here with you.'

'But you don't have to be here with me,' Cranfield told her. 'As you well know, it isn't a job requirement.'

'I like to make my own choices occasionally . . . though I never do it with men I might care for.'

'That puts me in my place.'

'Yes, Randolph, it does. You're my little convenience.'

Leaving him flushed with anger, she went into the bathroom, took her time showering, then returned to the bedroom and got dressed. As she was doing so he cooled down and soothed his wounded pride by watching her put her clothes on, piece by piece. It was as good as a striptease.

'Going back home could be dangerous,' he told her. 'You'd better be careful.'

'It won't be dangerous if you lift O'Leary out. In

that sense, his concerns are mine. I don't want him talkin'.'

'He's as good as gone,' Cranfield said.

Dressed and with hair combed, Margaret picked up her travel bag and walked up to the bed, where Cranfield was stretched out on top of the sheets, still completely naked.

'Are you stayin' here?' Margaret asked him.

'Only long enough to finish the wine,' he said, 'and get my breath back.'

She smiled, then leaned down to kiss him lightly on the lips. Straightening up, she said: 'You take care, Randolph.'

'I will,' Cranfield replied.

Margaret nodded and left the room.

Cranfield looked at his watch. Seeing that it was just after noon, he picked up the telephone. Calling a direct line to Lisburn HQ, he used a code-name that got him Captain Dubois.

'Cranfield here,' he said. 'What's happened at lunchtime?'

'A good lunch was had by all,' Dubois replied, 'and only one guest was missing.'

'Do you think it worth collecting him?' Cranfield asked, knowing that Dubois was referring to Michael Quinn.

'I think he has a lot to answer for,' Dubois replied, 'so you should go and fetch him.'

'Will do,' Cranfield said. Grinning like a Cheshire cat, he put down the receiver, hurried into the bathroom, showered, dressed and left the room – still carrying his Browning in the cross-draw position under the jacket of his immaculate pin-stripe suit.

Once outside the hotel, he caught a taxi to the Stanley Street RUC Station, by the Grosvenor Road, where a Q car, driven by Sergeant Lovelock, was waiting to take him to the lower Falls and Quinn's house.

'You got here just in time,' Sergeant Lovelock informed him as soon as he was in the car. 'Quinn's discovered the OP opposite his house and all hell's broken loose.'

'Damn!' Cranfield exclaimed softly, feeling fear for the first time, realizing, as the Q car shot out of the car park, that everything that could possibly go wrong was about to do so.

This time he had pushed his luck too far.

14

'I can smell something, I'm telling you,' Taff insisted, whispering, crouched up on the floor of O'Leary's loft and looking around him as if doubting his own sanity. 'I've smelt it for the last couple of days. It's the smell of . . .'

'You're just imagining it,' Lampton replied, also whispering. 'It's because we've been cooped up here so long. We haven't had a wash or a shave, we shit and piss in those plastic bags, and on top of all that, we haven't slept properly for days, so naturally we're inclined to think we can smell ourselves. You're just . . .'

'I don't think he's imagining it,' Gumboot said. 'I think I smell it as well.'

'Has anyone shit their pants?' Ricketts asked bluntly.

'No!' they all said in turn.

Ricketts glanced around the loft space, which remained surprisingly neat, considering how long the four of them had been secretly living up there. The Nikon F3HP heavy-duty camera with long-distance lens and D image intensifier, mounted on a tripod, was positioned just to the left of the peephole, being used only on special occasions. The STG laser surveillance system, tuned in to the probe in the wall adjoining Quinn's house across the street, was still at the peep-hole and working all the time, except when one of the men removed it temporarily to check the street or use the Thorn EMI 5kg hand-held thermal imager presently strung around Lampton's neck. Four sets of Gore-tex-lined Danner boots were standing in neat rows along one wall, as the need for silence had forced the men to remove them.

Even though they had been compelled to eat, wash, urinate and defecate up there, the wrappers from the only kind of food they had been able to have – the dry, high-calorie rations normally kept in their Escape Belts, such as biscuits, cheese, chocolate and sweets – as well as from moisturizing cloths, disposal towels and toilet paper, had been placed carefully in a large plastic bag hung from a nail on one of the walls and tied with string around the top. The vacuum flasks, now all empty, and water bottles, most of them nearly empty, were stacked neatly with the remainder of the rations in a noise-cushioning blanket in a corner of the loft. Most important, the sealed plastic bags for their excrement, urine and used toilet paper were in three larger plastic bags resting on the floor of the adjoining loft, which they had used as a toilet.

It was to the latter that Ricketts now cast his experienced eye.

'The bags?' he asked.

'They were all sealed after being used,' Gumboot said, 'and I personally examined every one of them.'

'Anyone piss and shit in the same bag?' Lampton asked over his shoulder while eyeballing the street through the peep-hole.

'No,' Gumboot said.

'No,' Ricketts added.

There was an uncomfortable silence for a moment, then Taff said: 'Oh, Jesus, I did that the first time . . . before you told us that we should keep them apart. Christ, I . . .'

'Piss and shit mixed can sometimes make the bags burst,' Lampton reminded them. 'I hope to God . . .'

'Damn!' Ricketts exclaimed softly, then hurriedly crossed the loft, at the crouch and stepping carefully from beam to beam, until he reached the adjoining space. There, he bent over, sniffed at the large bags, then checked the floor directly below them. A mixture of excrement and urine was dripping out of one of the rubbish bags, on to the floor. It was then dripping down between the joists and soaking through to the ceiling of the house below. 'Damn!' Ricketts exclaimed softly again. He turned back to look at the others, including the stricken Taff. 'One of the disposal bags has leaked and soaked through the floor to the ceiling of the room directly below, in the house next door. That'll give us away, I fear.'

'It already has,' Lampton replied, still at the peep-hole. 'One of the neighbours has just crossed from this side of the street – I think from the house next door – and is talking to Quinn. She's jabbing her finger in this direction.'

'Bloody 'ell!' Taff exclaimed softly. 'I didn't mean . . .'

'It's not your fault,' Lampton replied firmly. 'I should have told you about that deadly mixture before you used the first bag. My fault, Taff. My apologies, men.' He glanced through the peep-hole again, took a deep breath, then said: 'Yes, damn it, she's obviously told Quinn about the stain on her ceiling. He's just shouted into his own house, to call out a whole bunch of his hard men – four men. An ASU, no doubt. Yep, they all have guns. They're crossing the street to the house next door.' Lampton took another deep breath, then let it out again. 'Fuck! They've just gone out of view. That means they're entering the house.' Turning back to face his men, he said: 'Get on that radio, Gumboot, and call up a QRF to help bail us out of here. Ricketts, you keep the trapdoor in that next loft covered with your Browning. That's where they'll be coming up. But don't shoot unless someone aims at you – we don't want a riot. Taff, while Ricketts holds them at bay – which can only be temporary – you and I will have to pack up this equipment and have it ready for moving out. OK, men, shake out!'

Gumboot was already on the radio, calling for back-up from a QRF, or Quick Reaction Force, when Ricketts clambered over the joists to press his back against the bricks, raise his knees and aim his handgun two-handed at the trapdoor of the adjacent loft. Even before Lampton and Taff had begun dismantling and repacking the audiovisual surveillance equipment, Ricketts heard footsteps coming up the stairs from below, then the whispering of men on the landing directly below the trapdoor. Something clattered then squeaked – obviously a stepladder – prompting Ricketts to release the safety-catch of his Browning and hold the handgun firmly, applying pressure equally between the thumb and fingers of the firing hand. Waiting for the first man to appear, he took controlled, even breaths.

Completely ignoring Ricketts, Lampton and Taff got on with the business of dismantling the surveillance equipment and placing it back in reinforced canvas carriers. As they did so, Gumboot finished relaying his message to the Stanley Street RUC station, switched the set to 'Receive', then slithered sideways to glance down through the peep-hole. After noticing only that many of the neighbours were coming out of their homes to see what was happening, he withdrew his handgun and aimed it at the trapdoor in the adjoining loft, determined, on the one hand, to give covering to Ricketts, and on the other to keep his eye out for the arrival of the badly needed QRF.

The trapdoor squeaked, shook, then was suddenly flipped over by a human hand. A man's face appeared, his eyes too wide as they adjusted to the sudden gloom, then his second hand appeared, trying to aim his Webley.

'Halt!' Ricketts bawled. 'Security forces!'

A single shot from the man's pistol reverberated through the loft and the bullet ricocheted off the wall high above Ricketts's head. The man was firing wild and blind, but that made him no less dangerous, so Ricketts returned the fire with a double tap, which sounded like a deafening thunderclap in the confined space. The man's hand seemed to explode, spurting blood, bone and flesh. He screamed, dropped his pistol, then dropped back down through the trapdoor, knocking the steel ladder over as he crashed to the floor below. The other men down there cursed and bellowed instructions at one another. A woman further down screamed. Then a fusillade of pistol fire, shot vertically by the men below, straight up through the ceiling, turned the floor of the loft into a convulsion of spitting wood and billowing dust.

Ricketts pressed himself into the wall, then inched his way around it until he was closer to the open trapdoor. He leaned forward and emptied the rest of his 13-round magazine, aiming down through the trapdoor. There were more shouts and screams.

He pressed himself back against the wall and reloaded with a full magazine as the anticipated volley of return fire came from below, with the bullets smashing up through the floor in more spewing dust and wood chips, then ricocheting off the roof above his head. Even as Ricketts leaned forward to shoot down through the trapdoor hole again, Gumboot was inching forward with his High Power in one hand and a Royal Ordnance G60 stun grenade in the other.

Ricketts nodded.

Gumboot pulled the pin, dropped the grenade down through the hole, then threw himself back just as more shots were fired up through the ceiling. Dust and wood splinters spat up from the floor of the loft as the stun grenade exploded below with a loud bang and a blinding flash, leading to the cessation of the gunfire and a lot more cursing. Before the PIRA team could recover from the shock – for the stun grenade is essentially a diversionary device – Gumboot had shuffled forward again with another grenade in his hand.

'Smoke grenade,' he whispered.

Ricketts nodded again, then glanced at Lampton as Gumboot pulled the pin of the smoke grenade and dropped it down through the opening. Exploding almost instantly, the grenade filled the hallway below with smoke, which had everyone coughing even before it drifted up into the loft. Seeing what was happening, Lampton, who had just finished packing the surveillance equipment, nodded and picked up another canvas bag, from which he withdrew four SF10 respirators. When the men had put them on, to protect themselves from the smoke, which contained elements of burning CS gas, Lampton returned to the peep-hole, looked down on the street below, then stuck his thumb up in the air, indicating that the QRF force had arrived.

Wearing his respirator, and with his Browning ready to be fired single-handed, Ricketts moved forward to the opening and looked down into the smoke-filled hallway. The ladder was lying on its side where it had fallen, but otherwise the hallway was empty. From the ground floor, Ricketts could hear the hysterical babble of a woman – obviously the housewife – and more cursing and coughing from the PIRA men.

Ricketts dropped down through the hole and landed in the hallway just as gunshots were fired out in the street. He moved quickly along the passage, holding the Browning two-handed, kicking the two bedroom doors open, one after the other, and turning into the rooms ready to fire.

Both bedrooms were empty.

As Gumboot dropped down behind him, likewise wearing his respirator and holding his Browning two-handed, Ricketts hurried down the stairs, to the short hallway with the front door at one end and the living-room door to the side. As the door was open he went in, still preparing to fire. The room was empty, though filled with smoke and CS gas, so he checked the kitchen and back door, finding the latter locked. Satisfied that the house was empty, he hurried out to the hallway, just as Gumboot was pressing himself to the wall, his Browning still held two-handed, to tentatively stick his head around the door frame and look out into the street.

More gunshots rang out.

Gumboot disappeared outside and Ricketts followed him out, dropping low as he burst out of the front door, swinging the handgun from left to right, covering a wide arc. Women screamed, men hollered, and the spectators scattered. One woman was coughing and wiping her streaming eyes with a handkerchief, a man was squatting on the pavement with blood streaming from his head and shoulders – the results, so Ricketts surmised, of his own blind shots through the trapdoor hole – and a QRF team composed of British soldiers and RUC officers, all wearing flak jackets and carrying assault rifles and truncheons, were pouring out of Saracens to take command of the street.

Two other QRF teams had also arrived. One, consisting entirely of British Army troops, was rushing into O'Leary's house to help Lampton and Taff carry out their kit and equipment as quickly, and as securely, as possible. The other, composed of flak-jacketed RUC officers, was returning the gunfire of two PIRA men who were covering Quinn as he pushed the struggling O'Leary into the back of his car and followed him in with a pistol to his head. One of the PIRA gunmen managed to get into the car also, but the second was cut down as it roared off along the street and disappeared around the corner.

When the people saw the dead PIRA man, the feared riot began.

As the dead PIRA gunman was picked off the road by two RUC officers, the watching women started screaming abuse and the men — mostly youths, including some known dickers — started throwing stones and every other kind of debris. No sooner had they started than an armoured pig came along the street to disgorge special riot-control Army troops, wearing their familiar, still frightening flak jackets, perspex-visored helmets and reinforced leg and arm pads, who charged the crowd while holding up large shields and swinging their truncheons wildly.

Ricketts tugged the respirator off his face and let it hang loose just below his chin. Standing beside him, Gumboot did the same.

'Fuck it,' Gumboot said, 'they got O'Leary. They'll make that poor sod talk.'

'Let's protect the door,' Ricketts said.

Together they backed up to the door of O'Leary's house, since that was the one the QRF team had entered, probably under instructions. While stones and other debris drummed against the shields of the riot-control troops, who were now breaking up to swarm through the crowd and pick off certain individuals, Ricketts and Gumboot stood guard, both with their Brownings at the ready. Within minutes, even as the street battle raged, the soldiers who had rushed into O'Leary's house emerged again, this time in a protective circle around Lampton and Taff, both of whom were carrying packed-up surveillance equipment, as were some of the soldiers.

As Lampton and Taff were rushed to a waiting Saracen, a Q car pulled up and Lieutenant Cranfield climbed out, followed by Sergeant Lovelock. The latter was wearing a corduroy jacket and trousers, and an open-necked shirt. Cranfield was dressed in a black-leather jacket over what looked suspiciously like pinstripe trousers.

'Where's Quinn?' Cranfield asked.

Filled with a sudden, all-consuming rage, Ricketts raised his Browning, as if wanting to use it as a hammer, then walked purposefully up to Lieutenant Cranfield. Luckily, Lampton hurried back from the Saracen to push Ricketts back.

'That won't help,' he whispered.

'You heard the surveillance tapes,' Ricketts said. 'We both know what O'Leary did. We know what those PIRA fuckers'll do to him and who put him on that spot. We also know how many people will get hurt when O'Leary starts talking. We know who the big timer is.'

Ricketts started forward again, but again Lampton stopped him. 'One more move, Ricketts, and I swear I'll take *my* handgun and blow you to Kingdom Come. This won't wash. It's not your concern.'

'We're supposed to be the SAS,' Ricketts said. 'Not MI5.'

'I know,' Lampton said. 'Quiet now.' He turned to Cranfield, who took a step back and instinctively placed his hand inside his black-leather jacket, onto his Browning. 'Quinn got away,' Lampton said quietly, 'and he took O'Leary with him. He obviously guessed, from the location of our OP, that O'Leary had let us up there. He'll make him talk, Lieutenant.'

'It's time for a Chinese Parliament,' Cranfield replied, showing little emotion. 'Let's get the hell out of here.'

'Yes, boss,' Lampton said.

They all went their separate ways, heading back to Bessbrook in their own transport, leaving the QRF teams and riot-control soldiers to contain the continuing street violence.

The Saracen transporting Ricketts and Gumboot was stoned as it turned out of the street and headed back to Armagh.

'What a fucking war!' Gumboot said.

15

Cranfield knew he was in trouble as soon as he saw Captain Dubois' face. The Army intelligence officer was standing behind his desk, looking down through the window at the high-walled courtyard of Lisburn HQ, smoking a cigarette and radiating tension with every move of his body. When Cranfield entered the office, Dubois did not immediately turn to face him, but simply inhaled on his cigarette again, as if taking a deep breath to control himself.

Cranfield was already feeling shaky from the barrage of criticism he had received from, notably, Sergeant Lampton and Corporal Ricketts, at the Chinese Parliament, the informal meeting convened only an hour ago in the troop's sleeping quarters in Bessbrook.

Ricketts, in particular, had been incensed over what he had learnt about Cranfield's activities, from the conversations of Quinn and his spies, during his long surveillance in the OP above O'Leary's house. From those conversations, recorded over a period of five days, Ricketts and the others had learnt about Cranfield's illegal 'snatch' raids across the border, sometimes with, sometimes without, Captain Dubois; his killing of O'Halloran in his home in the Republic; and his exploitation of O'Leary's personal financial problems with PIRA.

Neither Ricketts nor Lampton were particularly concerned with the role of Dubois in all this, because Dubois was regular Army, not an SAS officer. They were, however, incensed that Cranfield, SAS, had overstepped the bounds of the Regiment's unwritten laws and, even worse, failed to consult any of his superiors before striking out on his own.

'It's out of order,' Sergeant Lampton had told him, 'and now we're paying the price for it. To the locals, we've become the new Black and Tans, while to the media we're a bunch of murderous cowboys. This is your fault, Lieutenant.'

As Cranfield knew only too well, regular Army officers entering the SAS for the first time invariably have to go through a painful period of adjustment when they discover that being limited to three-year stints deprives them of any real influence on the ethos of the Regiment; that the NCOs, who can remain in the Regiment for as long as their careers last, are actually the ones who will select or reject the officer entrants; and that even if selected, the officers will be treated with sly contempt by the NCOs and judged as short-term 'Ruperts' of dubious merit.

The SAS's Chinese Parliament, so alien to the regular Army, had sprung out of this unusual reversal of military rank and authority. They were, therefore, remarkably informal meetings – usually held before an operation, not after – at which everyone, from the commander down, could pitch in with his own ideas or criticisms. Apart from its recognition that the ordinary soldier can have as much to contribute as the officers, the Chinese Parliament is a regular, healthy reminder that the SAS scorns the notion of class.

While this attitude normally appealed to Cranfield, it had rebounded on him badly when, during that meeting, he had been so thoroughly lambasted by the contemptuous Lampton and Ricketts.

'You were grandstanding,' Sergeant Lampton had told him. 'Being a big timer. You wanted to fight this war on your own, but in the Regiment we work as a team. We're anonymous and you couldn't stand that, so you went out to be known. In doing that, you exposed us all.'

'Bullshit,' Cranfield had replied, trying to sound a lot more confident than he felt.

'No,' Ricketts had said. 'Not bullshit. Sergeant Lampton is right. It was your illegal snatch raids that brought you to the attention of Quinn and eventually made him go all-out to get you. That shouldn't have been the case. You should have played the game by the rules and remained anonymous, thus avoiding this range war with PIRA. It was also your cross-border raids that encouraged those dumb troopers on the Dublin road OP to pursue Quinn's arms dealers across the border, driving straight into a Gardai checkpoint, a highly publicized night in an Irish jail and subsequent deportation to Hereford. It's because of those men that Quinn learnt about the existence of the OPs overlooking his cottage in Armagh. And it's because of *that* discovery that Quinn learnt that we were after his hide and sent his men out to get us. Finally, it's because you insisted on inserting an OP facing Quinn's Falls Road home, in the house of your tout, O'Leary, that Quinn learnt he was helping us and took him away. When that poor bastard's tortured, he'll talk, blowing everything sky-high.'

'All of this, if I may say so,' Lampton had said icily, 'is because of your actions, which were based on self-interest and divorced from the best interests of the SAS.'

'We don't like big timers in this Regiment,' Ricketts had added, 'but that's what you were doing, Lieutenant – big timing all the way. Now the shit's hit the fan.'

Cranfield had argued his case, of course, but it hadn't cut much ice and when he left them it was with the knowledge that his reputation had been badly dented and possibly was now in ruins.

On the other hand, Lampton and Ricketts still

didn't know just how far he had gone to trap O'Leary in his web – namely, his use of Margaret Dogherty to get the Irishman in even more debt, thus encouraging him, with a little coaxing from Margaret, to turn to British Intelligence for financial assistance in return for information.

Thank God, they still didn't know about that.

Nevertheless, after that acrimonious, damning Chinese Parliament, Cranfield wasn't feeling too confident about this meeting with Captain Dubois. In fact, for the first time since childhood, he was feeling distinctly nervous. This feeling was not eased when Dubois turned around to face him, looking drawn and almost white with anger.

'Ah,' he said, sounding stiff. 'Lieutenant Cranfield!'

'Yes,' Cranfield said.

'Yes, *sir*!' Dubois corrected him.

'We use "boss" in the SAS.'

'You do realize, do you not, that although you're in the SAS, you come under the authority of the combined Intelligence and Security Group in this province?'

'Yes, boss, I realize that.'

'That means you must do as you're told. As an Army officer – your *senior* officer – I'm ordering you to address me as you would if in the regular Army. In other words, you address me as "sir".'

'Yes, sir,' Cranfield said, torn between anger and admiration for Dubois' surprising display of strength. Dubois, he suddenly realized, would have made a superb SAS officer. It made him like Dubois more.

Dubois nodded. 'You've taken a barrel of dynamite,' he said, 'and set a match to it. You've blown up the whole works. Do you understand that, Lieutenant?'

The use of his rank, instead of his first name, confirmed for Cranfield that Dubois was really, deeply upset with him. Nevertheless, unable to accept that he was wrong, he replied: 'No, I don't understand. I did what I thought was the best thing – and at least we've got Quinn on the run.'

'At what cost, Lieutenant?'

'Sorry?'

'The SAS is renowned not only for its skills in combat, but also for its use of psychological warfare when required – as it was in Malaya and Oman. The Regiment was brought here to use those same skills, but it made the mistake of bringing you with it, and what you've done, while very flamboyant, has caused more harm than good. Single-handedly you've destroyed the anonymity of the Regiment, risked the lives of a lot of other people, and set yourself up as PIRA's number one target, thus placing the SAS centre-stage. Do you understand now?'

'No,' Cranfield said. 'I think I've brought the worms out of the woodwork and given us a chance to get at them. Nothing comes without cost. I also think that I'm getting the blame for a lot of things I didn't do.'

Shaking his head in disbelief, Dubois took the chair behind his desk and folded his hands under his chin. He studied his desk for some time, then looked back up at Cranfield.

'This morning,' he said, 'another IRA terrorist, Sean McKee, in custody after being captured in south Armagh, supposedly by the RUC, claimed in court that in fact he'd been woken in his bed in the Republic by a British soldier holding a pistol to his head. That soldier, along with some of his friends, drove McKee back across the border and handed him over to the RUC. When the men responsible for this illegal act were named – and turned out to be some of your SAS troopers – they insisted that McKee was lying; that in fact he'd stumbled, drunk, into their foot patrol just this side of the border. McKee strongly denied this and stuck to his story, even as he was led away, thumbs defiantly in the air, to twenty-five years' imprisonment.'

Cranfield shrugged. 'McKee was high on a list of wanted men handed to us on our arrival in the area. We got him the only way we knew how.'

'The royal "we",' Dubois said sardonically.

Cranfield shrugged again. 'All right: I.'

Dubois nodded, then continued: 'With help from an informer, two others were arrested in the Republic and likewise handed over to the RUC – and again, the SAS was fingered.'

'I'm not responsible for them all,' Cranfield replied with his singular brand of sincerity. 'Some of my men are inclined to get impatient and take the initiative.'

'Having you as a bad example,' Dubois said.

'Naturally, I don't agree with that,' Cranfield said, holding his ground. 'And I really don't see how these cases, genuine though they are, can be used as examples of how I'm endangering the lives of other people. To join the SAS is to court danger – that's a weakness, or a perversion, shared by our officers, NCOs and troopers alike. So why blame me when what I do places my men in danger? It comes with the territory, Captain, so I've no guilt on that count.'

'Danger is one thing. *Unnecessary* danger is another, and that's what you brought about. Even worse, you didn't limit the danger to your SAS troopers; nor did you limit yourself to proper rules of engagement. Instead, you used a well-known local whore, Margaret Dogherty, to entrap that PIRA bookkeeper, Michael O'Leary, and make him turn into a Fred, doing so with scant regard for what might happen, should the couple be caught out.'

Cranfield opened his mouth to protest, but Dubois silenced him with a pointing index finger, then continued: 'Even worse, having already ignored the danger, in particular to O'Leary, you then offered him a lift-off to Australia in return for the use of his house for a covert OP – one inserted to watch the very man who could do O'Leary most damage, namely Michael Quinn. In doing so, you practically guaranteed that O'Leary's turn would be exposed – and in doing *that* you also virtually guaranteed that all those connected with O'Leary would be taken down with him. In the event, that's what happened.'

Suddenly, Cranfield felt his blood turning cold, some instinct telling him that he was about to hear something he would never forget.

'O'Leary's body has already been picked up from waste ground near the Divis flats,' Dubois said. 'First they gave him a six-pack with a pistol – elbows, kneecaps and ankles. Then they dropped concrete blocks on his shins. Then, while he was pinned down by the concrete blocks, they put a plastic bag over his head, kicked his ribs in, tortured him with a knife; and finally, presumably when he had talked, they blew his brains out. You can tear up his ticket to Australia – it's no use to him now.'

Suddenly feeling light-headed, Cranfield closed his eyes, took a deep breath and tried to control the racing of his heart. Realizing that this might be misconstrued as a sign of weakness, he opened his eyes again and said, as calmly as he could manage: 'O'Leary did what he did of his own accord and for his own benefit. He took his chances and paid the price. We all run that risk.'

There was silence for much longer than Cranfield could take comfortably, but eventually Captain Dubois, after another loud sigh, said: 'Yes, I suppose so. There's a certain truth in that. If you hadn't gotten to him first, his theft from the PIRA funds would have been discovered anyway, resulting in something rather similar to his ultimate fate.' He paused deliberately, tormentingly, but eventually added with chilling softness: 'We'll conveniently ignore the fact that your way of helping O'Leary out was to force him into becoming a turncoat. He was, after all, a member of PIRA and therefore, in the strictest sense of the term, still one of the enemy.'

'Correct,' Cranfield said, instantly feeling better.

'Unfortunately,' Dubois continued with soft-voiced, remorseless logic, 'that doesn't absolve you from the charge that your exploitation of O'Leary, and subsequent carelessness regarding him, put the lives of a lot of others in danger.'

'If you're talking about the OPs,' Cranfield said, already getting his confidence back, 'I'd remind you that they were manned by the SAS – and those men *expect* danger.'

'Not danger brought about by carelessness.'

'The use of that word is debatable.'

'Then what about the many others who might have been exposed by what O'Leary has revealed under torture?'

'What others?'

'The many who passed him information or were party to your entrapment and subsequent use of him.'

'Such as?'

'Let's suggest Margaret Dogherty. The woman with whom you've been having an affair . . .'

'You've had me watched?' Cranfield asked, taken by surprise, shocked, and flushed with anger.

'Of course. We keep our eye on our own men – particularly when they're involved in clandestine surveillance.'

'You bastard!'

'And in doing so,' Dubois continued with a slight, deadly smile, 'we learnt of your affair with Miss Dogherty. As that lady had already worked for us in London and Dublin, we weren't amused to find you becoming involved with her, far beyond the call of duty. It was completely out of order. Even more out of order, if I may say so, was getting her killed.'

The shock jolted through Cranfield like a bolt of electricity, first burning him, then turning him to ice, finally leaving him numb, with only a racing heart to remind him that he was still made of flesh and bone.

'What . . .?' He had to take a deep breath and let the word out when exhaling, but he simply couldn't finish his question, already dreading the answer.

'When O'Leary was tortured,' Dubois said with deadly calm, 'he must have confessed to pilfering the PIRA money. In doing so, he would also have told them that Margaret Dogherty had introduced him to you and that you had offered to replace the money if he became your tout. Given that Margaret Dogherty was, for reasons known to all the locals, not sympathetic to the local PIRA, who had once feathered and tarred her, Michael Quinn and his hoodlums would soon have put two and two together and gone in search of the lady, seeking revenge.'

Cranfield felt that he was choking, or about to be ill, but he managed to croak out: 'So what . . .?'

'We received the call this afternoon. She was shot in her own home. She was looking after her terminally ill mother when the men rang her doorbell. When she answered it, they emptied their pistols into her, killing her instantly. At the same time, all across the city, other people were murdered – seven in all. Our records show that they were all connected with O'Leary – and through him, to us.' Dubois paused, then offered his penultimate, lacerating statement: 'Yes, O'Leary talked . . . and nine people died. Congratulations, Lieutenant.'

Cranfield didn't ask permission to leave. He just did an abrupt about-turn and walked to the door, not sure if his legs would carry him there. In the event, they did. As he opened the door and started out, he was stopped by Dubois' voice.

'You've not only done irreparable damage to yourself, but also to the whole SAS. This time, if you try to make amends, don't make a mistake.'

'Go to hell,' Cranfield said.

Then he walked out, slamming the door behind him, determined to find Quinn.

16

Darkness had fallen when Cranfield, dressed in mismatching civilian clothing, including baggy brown-corduroy trousers, scuffed black shoes, threadbare coat, open-necked checkered shirt and stained navy-blue pullover, drove out of Bessbrook in a Q car, heading for the border.

His Browning was holstered to the side of his right leg and a Fairburn-Sykes Commando knife was strapped to the other, both up under his trousers.

Soon he was driving ever deeper into the country, along narrow, winding lanes lined with high hedgerows. Given the fiasco of this whole day, including the Chinese Parliament and his meeting with Dubois, he knew that what he was doing was a final, desperate gamble that would either redeem him or destroy him. Nevertheless, so great was his present humiliation that he felt he had finally to get Quinn or concede victory to him.

Lambert and Ricketts, he knew, would be even more infuriated if they discovered that he had struck out on his own again – and, even worse, taken another dangerous chance – but Cranfield just didn't give a damn, since apart from the humiliations already heaped upon him, not least by Lampton and Ricketts, he now had to contend with Dubois' parting shot: 'This time, if you try to make amends, don't make a mistake.'

Well, Cranfield thought grimly, *if I make a mistake this time I won't live long enough to be haunted by it. This time it's for keeps.*

Stopped once by an Army foot patrol, he showed his genuine identity papers and was allowed to drive on. Soon after, he was parking his unmarked car outside a Republican bar located halfway between the border and Quinn's cottage. It was a picturesque little place, with leaded-glass windows, now emitting light from inside, doors of solid oak, and a thatched roof. Smoke was coming out of its single chimney, indicating that an open fire was burning. When Cranfield rolled down the window of his car, he heard the distinctive sound of Irish music coming from inside.

Although Quinn would certainly not be found in this pub, it was one he had frequented during his visits to south Armagh, and therefore one in which he had many friends. Cranfield hoped to pick something up from them, then take it from there. It was a hellishly dangerous thing to attempt, but he felt he had no choice. He would not return to Bessbrook empty-handed. The very thought was unbearable.

After turning off the ignition and headlights, he took his genuine ID from his inside pocket and slipped it under the rubber mat on the floor. He then checked that his false ID was still in his inside pocket and double-checked his wallet, making sure that it contained only false credit cards and other personal items, with nothing that might give him away as an Englishman. According to his false ID, credit cards and even a letter from an invented mother, he was Bobby Duncan from Balkan Street, Belfast – a hard Republican street.

Satisfied, Cranfield climbed out of the car, locked it, took a few deep breaths, then walked across the gravelled forecourt and entered the pub. It was small, warm and noisy, with a beamed ceiling, a brass-and-wood bar, a four-piece Irish band – autoharp, fiddle, flatpick guitar, mandolin and singer – a postage-stamp dance floor, already busy, and pink-faced men and women packed into seats around the walls, drinking, smoking, talking, and joining the singer as chorus on patriotic songs.

Nobody stopped what they were doing when Cranfield walked in, but he sensed a lot of eyes turning towards him and tried to ignore them. Walking to the bar, he said with an Ulster brogue: 'A lively wee place you've got here. Sure I picked a good place to stop off. Pour me a Guinness, thanks.' Turning to the man beside him, he said: 'Sure it warms the belly all of a winter's night. It's quare good when yer travellin'.'

'Aye,' the man replied, smoking his pipe and puffing a cloud of blue smoke. 'Sure that's a fact, Mister. Ya be just passin' through then?'

'On m' way back to Belfast from Dublin after one of them ijit sales conventions. I'm in linens, like. A grand place, that Dublin, but quare expensive. I'll be glad to get back t' Balkan Street an' put m'feet up.'

'Sure there's nothin' like home'n hearth,' the man replied, blowing another cloud of smoke across the bar. 'I'd say that's a fact of life.'

The barman placed Cranfield's Guinness on the counter. Cranfield thanked him, paid, had a good drink, then engaged the man beside him in conversation.

'Sure that's a quare wee band they have up there. And that singer's real grand.'

'Ach, he's not bad. Gets them all goin' at it. By closin' time they'll have to read the Riot Act. It's a right wee place, this 'un.'

'Ach, it is,' Cranfield said. 'Sure I'm havin' a grand time already.'

Cranfield was proud of his Ulster accent and vernacular, but knowing it wasn't perfect, he was depending on the general, noisy level of conversation to hide any slight mistakes he might make. 'Here,' he said to the man beside him. 'Let me get you another. I'm Bobby Duncan, by the way.'

'Sure that's quare decent of you, Bob.' The man stuck his hand out. 'Mick Treacy.' They shook hands, then Cranfield ordered the man a Guinness. The singer had stopped singing and was telling a few jokes while the fiddler tuned up behind him. The men and women in the pub roared with laughter at the jokes, their faces flushed with drink and good humour. 'In the palm of his hand,' Cranfield said. 'Sure 'e knows what 'e's doin'.'

'Aye, he's a rare turn,' Mick replied. 'Alus good for a laugh. Lives local, like.'

'You'd all be locals here,' Cranfield said.

'All exceptin' the odd traveller like yerself. It's not a place you'd seek out.'

The band started up again, with the singer launching into 'Provie Birdie', a song about three Provos who, in real life, were lifted out of Mountjoy prison by helicopter, right under the noses of the guards. It was clear from the number of customers who joined in the chorus that the song was widely known and popular.

While engaging the amiable Mick in conversation, Cranfield sipped his Guinness and studied the smoky pub over the rim of his glass. The customers were a mixture of heavy housewives, working men in peaked caps, a few country-squire types, and, at the bar, on both sides of Cranfield, single men, most edging towards middle age. The younger men, most of whom were not too bright and undoubtedly in the Provisionals, had congregated along the pine-board wall between the bar and the door and were being fêted by teenage girls attracted to the excitements of terrorism. It was the young men, trying to impress the girls, who acted most like hard men and looked with blatant suspicion upon strangers. Seeing them, and the sideways glances they gave him, Cranfield sensed trouble.

'Sure have another Guinness on me,' Mick said as Cranfield turned back to face the bar. 'With perhaps a wee Bushmills.'

'That sounds great,' Cranfield said.

The round led into a second, helping to pass the next hour, then a friend of Mick's joined them at the bar and insisted on buying a third round. Conversation flowed thick and fast, bouncing from one subject to another, though most of it was about the Troubles in Belfast, Londonderry and south Armagh. The 'Brits' were reviled as bastards, but deemed ignorant rather than evil. Opinions about the IRA, its vices and virtues, were surprisingly varied.

The latter fact surprised Cranfield, as he had expected more unanimity in favour of the IRA — based on fear of reprisals, if nothing else — but everyone seemed to have his own opinion and felt free to air it.

The arguments grew more lively, the band played ever louder, the husbands and wives along the walls continued to sing uninhibitedly, and soon all conversations were being shouted from flushed, sweaty faces, through blue-grey veils of swirling cigarette smoke.

Eventually, just before closing time – which, as Cranfield knew, meant closing only the front door – the name of Michael Quinn was finally raised.

'Sure, the Troubles could be on yer doorstep,' Cranfield said, 'and you wouldn't even be knowin' it. At least not here in the country. Not like in the Falls.'

'Ach, aye,' Mick replied, polishing off a quick Bushmills. 'Take that incident yesterday – that to-do at Michael Quinn's place. Sure you never see the man hereabouts, 'cept on weekends, and then the Brits shoot up the place, killin' some lads into the bargain, and find the walls stacked high with weapons, ammunition an' s'plosives. Enough to blow up this whole village, so I've heard. Sure, it makes yer hair stand on end, it does.'

'Killed some lads, did they?' Cranfield asked rhetorically. 'Sure them bastards would kill their own mothers.'

'Aye, they would,' Mick replied, 'but they didn't get Quinn. It's been said he was in the Falls at the time an' didn't know what was goin' on.'

'Didn't know, my arse!' It was Mick's friend Kevin talking. 'That stuff didn't get into Quinn's house by accident. He had to know what was goin' on.'

'A lot of poor lads kilt.'

'All Provos,' Kevin said. 'As for Quinn, he was hidin' out there in the Falls until the milit'ry went for him.'

'Did they catch him?' Cranfield asked.

'Sure he took off like a bat out of hell an' hasn't been seen since. Ask me, he's hidin' out in Sean Doyle's house, just two miles down the road. That's the safe house he alus used for his PIRA mates, so that's where he'd stop first.'

Mick sighed. 'Sure you could be right there. As Bobby said' – Mick beamed a big smile at Cranfield – 'the Troubles could be right on yer doorstep and you wouldn't even know it. Aye, he could be right there in Doyle's place.'

'Let them British bastards worry about it,' Cranfield said. 'It's their concern, not ours.' He glanced at his watch and looked shocked. 'Bejasus! It's near midnight already! Me missus will kill me if I don't get back soon. Sorry, lads, but I'm goin' t' have t' go. What a quare good night that was.' He finished off his Guinness, shook hands all round, then had the usual trouble saying goodbye in Ireland, but finally managed it.

'You drive carefully now,' Mick advised him. 'Sure you've had a right few.'

'Ach, I'll be all right,' Cranfield said, waving again and heading for the door. 'Sure we salesmen are used t' this. Good night, Mick.'

'God bless.'

Gratefully leaving the bar, with his stomach tightening but excitement lancing through him, Cranfield hurried back across the dark courtyard to his parked Q car.

He was about to open the door when a young man stood up, where he had been kneeling at the other side, and aimed a Webley pistol held with both hands.

'Bobby Duncan, my arse,' he said.

Before Cranfield could think of what to do, he heard the scuffle of many feet behind him. Glancing back over his shoulder he saw the youths from the pub hurrying towards him – at least six or seven of them. Cranfield just had time to return his gaze to the youth aiming the pistol at him – long unwashed hair, fashionable 'designer' stubble, hollow cheeks, eyes shadowed; wearing a black leather jacket and blue denims – then the other youths rushed up to surround him. One of them pushed him in the face. Another flung him forward face first against the car, brutally punched his spinal column, kicked his ankles apart and snarled: 'Open those fuckin' legs, you English cunt!'

Cranfield did as he was told. The first youth frisked him, running his hands over his shoulders, down his chest, across his stomach, around his waist, up his spine, then back around his body to reach in and pull out his wallet.

'No weapon,' he said. 'Fuckin' amazin'! Let's see what we have here. Hey, you, turn aroun'!'

Before Cranfield could do so, someone grabbed him by the hair, jerked his head back, slapped his face, then grabbed his shoulder, spun him around and slammed him backwards into the car, letting him see all their faces. They were definitely the youths he had seen inside the pub — deprived, not too bright, clearly desperate for self-esteem — and all of them shared the same smirk of combined hatred and nervousness.

One of them, the one who'd reached Cranfield first, was examining his wallet.

'I don't fuckin' believe it,' he exclaimed, turning over Cranfield's false ID, credit cards and varied papers to examine them thoroughly. 'This bastard is genuine!'

'No, he's not,' a more mature, familiar voice said. 'He's just a Brit tryin' t' be clever. Let's check his car.'

Glancing over the shoulder of the youth with his wallet, Cranfield saw the amiable Mick Treacy. Returning Cranfield's stare, he said: 'You think I'm a fuckin ijit, you British turd? *Good night*, indeed! Who says "good night" around here? You were good, Mister, at playin' an Ulsterman, but not *that* fuckin' good. OK, lads, get 'is car keys.'

'In my right trouser pocket,' Cranfield said, since he had nothing to lose.

'Well, isn't he a quare wee lad?' Mick said sarcastically as one of the youths jammed his hand into Cranfield's pocket and pulled out his keys. 'So helpful an' all! They breed the wee uns like that in the Falls Road — as polite as the English. Right, Jim-boy, search the car.'

The youth with the Webley pistol walked around the car, grabbed Michael by the shoulder, dragged him off a few feet, and slammed him backwards into the trunk of a tree. Then he placed the barrel of the pistol against his forehead, right above the bridge of the nose.

'One fuckin' move and you get it. Not one tremor, cunt.'

Cranfield remained against the tree, trying to keep his breathing steady, but unable to stop the racing of his heart as the youths searched his Q car. They did it thoroughly, with growing excitement, as if doing even that turned them on and encouraged their violence. One opened the glove compartment, another searched through the back, two more checked the cluttered boot, one looked under the bonnet. Finding nothing, they became frustrated, smashing windows, slashing the seats, until finally, to Cranfield's despair, one of them ripped the rubber mat away and saw the ID beneath it.

He picked the ID up. After examining it with the aid of a pencil torch, he walked across to Mick and handed it to him.

'Fucking British Army,' he said. 'You were right again, Mick.'

'Mmmmm,' Mick said, examining the ID, then looking directly at Cranfield and offering a slight smile. 'Sure the Troubles could be on yer doorstep and you wouldn't even be knowin' it,' he

repeated sardonically. 'Isn't that the truth, Lieutenant Cranfield? Now we have the proof of it.
After Michael Quinn, were ya?'

'Yes,' Cranfield said.

'Well, let's not disappoint ya.'

When Mick nodded at the gang of youths, they
closed in on Cranfield, some grinning like idiots,
others breathing deeply, all of them excited to be
given something worthwhile to do. They punched
him and kicked him, head-butted him, spat on him,
tore his clothes, tugged at his hair and trampled on
his toes. When he started falling, they held him
up; when they had him upright, they punched
him down; and when finally he could stand up
no longer, they used their boots on him.

At first Cranfield felt sharp pain – each single
blow, every kick – then the jolting, individual
bolts of pain spread out through him to become
a generalized agony that throbbed throughout his
whole being. When he finally collapsed, stretched
out on grass and gravel, where they kicked the hell
out of him, his nausea overwhelmed the pain and
made him throw up.

'God!' a youth said in disgust, then kicked
Cranfield as punishment. 'Puked over m'boots!
Take that you filthy English bastard!' Cranfield
was kicked again and rolled over to look up at the
stars, his head filled with a dreadful, tightening pain
as his vision blurred badly.

'Right, lads, that's enough,' the amiable Mick

Treacy said. 'Let's get him into the van . . . Jim-boy, you've still got his keys?'

'Yeah, Mick.'

'Then drive his car away to where we can best make use of it later on. Sure this git won't be needin' it.'

Only dimly aware of what was happening, Cranfield was thrown into the back of the van, landing in a mess of tyres, tools and rope, then followed in by most of the youths. Mick Treacy sat up front beside the youth who had examined Cranfield's wallet and was now their driver.

'Quickly now,' Treacy told him.

The journey did not take long. Slowly getting his senses back, feeling battered and bruised, Cranfield reasoned that the safe house hiding Quinn was indeed only two miles away. Certainly, after rattling and bouncing over what was obviously a crude, country track, the van finally arrived at its destination and ground to a halt.

When the back doors were opened, most of the youths climbed out. Cranfield was picked up by the two remaining, dragged halfway out, then thrown off the back of the van. Hitting the ground, he almost cried out with the pain, but managed to stifle it. He was picked up again, punched two or three times, then dragged across grassy earth, on to a strip of gravel, and finally through the front door of a small cottage, into a warm, brightly lit room.

Picked up a third time, he was placed on a hard

wooden chair. His arms were pulled roughly, pain-fully, over the back of the chair, then his wrists and shoulders were strapped to it. His ankles were tied to the legs of the chair – luckily, the ropes were just above the ankles, well below the holstered gun and knife, which were not detected – then the youths stepped away to smirk at him.

A man who had been sitting in an armchair in front of the open fire, stood up, walked forward and stopped in front of him.

The man had a head of healthy grey hair and a hard, angry face.

'Who's this?' he asked Mick Treacy while looking at Cranfield.

Mick handed the man Cranfield's ID. The man studied it at length, first thoughtfully, then incredulously, finally with a thin, cruel smile. He leaned down to Cranfield, studied him intently, then slapped his face with his own ID and said: 'Lieutenant Cranfield of the fucking SAS! Sure isn't this a pleasant wee surprise! And you look just like yer picture.'

'What picture?' Cranfield asked, getting his senses back and desperate to hear the sound of his own voice, which might help calm his growing fears. 'You mean on the ID?'

Again the man slapped Cranfield's face with the ID, saying: 'No, I don't mean this shit. Sure we had yer photo taken by some of our own boyos and I've had many a good gander at it. I'd recognize you,

Lieutenant, with yer feet stickin' out of a barrel. Sure it's a pleasure to meet you.'

'You're Michael Quinn,' Cranfield said, trying to keep his voice steady.

'The one an' only,' Quinn replied. He studied Cranfield's ID, nearly threw it into the fire, changed his mind and carefully put it back into Cranfield's jacket pocket. 'By the time we finish with you they won't recognize you, so you might as well have some identification.' He straightened up to grin first at Mick Treacy, then at the assembled youths. 'So what'ya think of the brave SAS lieutenant?'

One of them spat in Cranfield's face and said: 'Whoever had this bastard would drown nothin'.'

'A mother's love is blind,' Mick Treacy informed him. 'You'll learn that when yer older.'

Some of the youths laughed nervously. Michael Quinn just smiled. It was a smile that made Cranfield feel more frightened that he'd imagined he could be.

It's not real, he thought desperately. *Stay calm. Don't make any mistakes. It all depends on what you say or don't say, so don't let them trick you. Don't panic. Don't break.*

'So what where ya doin' in my pub?' Quinn asked. 'Apart from havin' the Guinness. Lookin' for me, were you?' When Cranfield didn't immediately reply, Quinn slapped him viciously with the back of his hand, then said, 'Well, were you?'

'Yes,' Cranfield said.

Quinn straightened up, looking pleased. 'Why?'

Cranfield found it hard to breathe. 'I think you know why,' he replied.

'Gonna put a British bullet into my head. Was that what you were plannin'?' When Cranfield didn't reply, Quinn slapped him again and said, 'Well, was it?'

'Yes,' Cranfield said.

'Now why would ya want to be doin' that? Was it because of O'Leary?'

'My name is Randolph Cranfield,' Cranfield said. 'My rank is . . .'

Quinn's hand pressed over his mouth and pushed his head back until the wood of the hard chair was chopping painfully into his neck.

'When we want your name, rank, serial number and date of birth we'll ask for it,' Quinn said. Removing his hand, he continued: 'It was O'Leary. Sure don't I know that, Lieutenant? You came to get me for what I did to that weak, treacherous shite. Well, O'Leary's dead and buried, Lieutenant, an' he sang like a bird. That's why him and his whore were killed – along with a bunch of other shites. He was a tout, a turncoat, your wee Fred, so he had to be put down.'

'You could have just killed him,' Cranfield said. 'You didn't have to . . .'

Quinn's fist smashed into his face, making his head explode with pain. When he recovered, he found it difficult to breathe and felt blood on his face. Quinn had broken his nose.

'Of course we had to,' Quinn said. 'He had a mouth like a torn pocket. Every time he opened his mouth he took a wrong step. What was wrong was right for us and he sang like a canary. He gave us a lot of important names and made our hearts leap for joy. Now what about Margaret Dogherty?'

'My name is . . .'

Quinn pressed the palm of his hand against Cranfield's broken nose and squeezed until even Cranfield couldn't hold back the tears nor prevent himself screaming. When Quinn thought he'd had enough, he removed his hand and smiled a thin smile. 'You and her were thick, were you?'

'We shared a bed a few times,' Cranfield acknowledged, though he found breathing difficult.

'You'll be sharin' a fucking grave with her soon,' Quinn responded, 'though you won't be goin' as quick as she did. Twelve bullets she had in 'er. From the guns of two men. She went quicker than the clap of a duck's wing. You should be so lucky.'

'Fuck you,' Cranfield said.

Quinn punched him so hard that the chair went over backwards and the back of his head smashed into the floor. Pains darted across his forehead, exploded behind his nose, spread out across the back of his head, and shot down from his shoulder blades to his pinioned arms. He was temporarily blinded – by tears as well as pain – when someone pushed the chair upright again, returning him to the sitting position, where his breathing was anguished.

'I don't think he's feeling too well,' Mick Treacy said.

'Ach, he'll be all right when he's better,' Quinn replied. 'Sure he belongs to the SAS. A quare bunch of boys they are.' He leaned forward, no longer smiling, and stared directly into Cranfield's weeping eyes. 'We don't want yer fucking name, rank, serial number or date of birth. What we want is a lot of information about you and your friends in British Intelligence. We ask. You answer. Is that understood?'

'My name is . . .'

The pain was excruciating, exploding from his genitals, almost too much to bear yet becoming even worse when Quinn squeezed his testicles even harder. Cranfield screamed without thinking. He almost came off the chair, but was held down by the ropes. He would have lifted the chair off the floor, but one of the youths held him down. When Quinn released him, letting the pain subside a little, he could not stop the shaking of his body nor stem the pouring of sweat.

'What do you expect?' Quinn asked rhetorically. 'You want mercy, Lieutenant? Yer thinkin' I can't be that bad and won't go any further? Well, don't kid yourself, you ijit. I'll do more than you can imagine. I've lost two childern and a lot of friends to the Brits an' been tortured myself. First Crumlin Road jail. Then fucking Long Kesh. The Brits have their own wee ways in there – and none of 'em pleasant. Mercy, Lieutenant? Sure I'm not interested. I could have stayed sane in Long Kesh if I'd had children to think about, but my childern were killed by British bullets in what was classed as an accident. Of course I still had a wife. We used to live in Conway Street. We were there in sixty-nine when the Prods wrecked the place while the RUC looked the other way. Our house was fire-bombed. My children were in hysterics. A Prod with a baseball bat that had nails stickin' out of it smashed my missus over the head an' ran off down the street. My missus died that day. She became someone else. She was so crazed, she terrified the kids an' they had to take 'er away. Then the British Army took over, searched our houses, controlled our streets. They swore at our women, fired rubber bullets at our children, and treated us as if we were animals, only fit for the slaughterin'. One day, when they weren't firin' rubber bullets, they fired at my kids, killin' both of them outright. They said it was an accident, the bastards, an' left it at that. But I didn't. I won't. So don't ask me for mercy. You came here to put a bullet through my head, but instead you'll just talk. You know the Irish, don't you? We all like to talk – a good bit of crack to pass the time – so start talkin', Lieutenant. If you don't, we have our own wee ways. Now here's the first question . . .'

'My name is . . .'

There is pain and there is pain, some of which is beyond describing. What Cranfield endured over the next few hours was beyond comprehension. He heard his own screaming, reverberating through his head. It wasn't a sound that he recognized as his own, but it opened doors that led into hell. There were punches and kicks. Sharpened blades cut through to bone. The first gunshot, which filled the room like thunder, took his kneecap away.

'God,' Cranfield gasped, licking his tears from his upper lip as they dripped from his dazed eyes down his cheeks. 'My name is . . .'

He lost a second kneecap. The gun's roaring, which was deafening, did not drown out his screaming, which seemed to reverberate through his head to leave it ringing and spinning. At some point he vomited. He then dry-retched for some time. His stomach was in knots and his heart was racing, waiting for the next torment.

He smelt it before he felt it. Burning flesh and bodily hair. They stubbed their cigarettes out on his chest, against his nipples, in his ears, then a cigarette lighter was ignited and held under his nostrils.

Pain became his whole world.

It's not real, he thought, trying to stop himself from shivering, trying to choke back his vomit, determined in some buried cell of himself to hold on to his dignity. *Bear in mind that nothing is real, that nothing can break you. Just don't make a mistake.*

'My name is . . .'

Finally, he was on the floor, rolling about on the tiles, not feeling the cold because he was burning, immunized by the pain to the hardness, floating out of himself. There is pain and there is pain, he now knew, but there was none he had not felt.

'Sure I'll give you this,' Quinn said, standing over him and kicking his broken ribs with no great deal of hope, 'you're one tough, tight-lipped, determined bastard. A man has to admire that.'

'So what now?' Mick Treacy asked.

'Do you think this bag of shit and piss will talk?'

'He's beyond talkin', Michael.'

'Then let's take 'im out and put an end to 'im an' we'll still come out winners.'

'Achay, that's the ticket! Let's make fertilizer out of the shite an' help Ireland's green grass grow.'

'Hood 'im,' Quinn said.

A hood was slipped over Cranfield's head and tightened around his neck with a cord, making him feel claustrophobic and totally blind. A spasm of terror whipped through him, then passed away again.

Breathe deeply and evenly, he thought. *You're not going to choke. They're just trying to panic you.*

They picked him off the floor, forgetting about his smashed kneecaps. When he screamed and started falling again, they cursed and let him fall, then caught him by the shoulders and dragged him backwards across the brightly lit room. Someone opened the front door, letting freezing air rush in, then they dragged him across the dark courtyard and threw him back into the van. When he hit the tyres, tools and ropes, practically bouncing off the former, his smashed knees exploded with more pain and his broken ribs screamed – or he screamed – or some animal screamed.

That wasn't me, he decided.

'Don't vomit,' Mick Treacy said helpfully, 'or you'll just choke t' death. Sure it's real messy, that is.'

The van kicked into life and trundled off the forecourt. It bounced a little, then turned on to the narrow road that led into the countryside. The journey, which seemed to take for ever, took only a few minutes. The van stopped in a lay-by at the foot of a gentle hill. The wind moaned through the trees.

'Sure this is as good as any place,' Mick said in his amiable way. 'Let's drag the sack of spuds out.'

'Right,' Quinn said, 'let's do that.'

They dragged Cranfield to the rear of the van, then just rolled him off the edge. He hit the ground with a thud and let his scream wipe out the pain, then he felt the ground under his stomach and thighs as they dragged him across a stretch of sharp stones and eventually on to wet grass. It was easier on the grass, less painful, though cold, and he knew that he was being dragged uphill, out into the windy field.

When they'd dragged him another ten yards or so, they released him again. He fell face down in the grass, then rolled on to his back.

'Sit up,' Quinn said.

Cranfield took a deep breath, tried to sit up, but fell back. A youth cursed and grabbed him by the shoulders and propped him upright. Cranfield was finding it hard to breathe, but he clung to his dignity.

'I don't need the hood,' he said.

There was silence for a moment, as if they were deciding, then eventually the cord around his throat was loosened and the hood was tugged off.

He saw Quinn's healthy head of grey hair and his hard, angry face. Behind him were the amiable Mick Treacy and two of the youths. All of them were holding Webley pistols. All were aiming at him. The wind was howling across the dark field and there were stars in the cloudy sky.

'That's the only kind of mercy you'll get,' Michael Quinn told him. 'Do you have any last words?'

Cranfield thought of his wife and children, his many years in the army, his more admirable days with the SAS and all it had taught him. He hadn't completely failed. He'd just made a few mistakes. As Lampton and Ricketts had said, he'd big-timed too many times; but for all that, he'd done a good job and had only one left to do. He didn't know that it was possible to do it now, but he would certainly try.

'Fuck off,' he said.

Quinn kicked him in the ribs and cracked his head with his pistol, making him fall back and roll a few feet back down the hill, deeper into the darkness.

'Fuckin' British shite!' Quinn said, then started forward.

Cranfield rolled farther away and tugged his trouser leg up. He grabbed the Browning, jerked it out of its holster, and rolled on to his back to aim it two-handed at Quinn as he advanced with his pistol raised.

Quinn stopped, eyes widening, and started aiming his pistol, even as Cranfield fired his first shots in a precise double tap.

Quinn was stopped dead in his tracks, jolting as if electrocuted. He jerked back as if tugged on a string and thudded into the earth.

Even before Quinn hit the ground, Cranfield was swinging the handgun elsewhere, managing to put a burst into Mick Treacy before the two youths returned his fire.

He saw Treacy step backwards, a surprised look on his face, then the bullets from the Webleys smashed his chest and made his insides explode.

He saw stars between the clouds, then the stars, then a big star, then a white light.

Cranfield died in that radiance.

17

The news came into Bessbrook just after Cranfield's men had left the base for a raid on a housing estate in the Falls.

Captain Dubois had been informed by the 'green slime' that a couple of IRA men were being hidden in the estate and preparing to snipe on a British Army foot patrol. Short of his own soldiers, he had hauled the SAS troop out of their bashas at first light and told them to prepare for an assault. They were on the road within ten minutes, but without Lieutenant Cranfield, who hadn't been seen since storming out of Dubois' office the previous afternoon.

When the telephone rang, Dubois, wondering where Cranfield had gone this time, though certainly suspecting what he was up to, was watching the armoured pig containing the SAS troops leaving its parking bay below. He turned away from the window, picked up the phone, and listened to the person speaking on the other end of the line, first with disbelief, then with growing awareness, and inally with a look of deep thoughtfulness.

'And you're sure one of the dead men was Quinn?'

'Yes,' his caller, an RUC officer, said. 'The bodies were brought back and positively identified.'

'Excellent,' Dubois said. 'Thank you.'

He put the phone down and returned to the window just as the armoured pig left through the guarded gates of the compound, heading for Belfast.

'Well, well,' Dubois whispered to himself, 'he actually did it. It worked!' Returning to his desk, he picked up the phone, dialled HQ Lisburn, and used a code-name to get his MI5 associate. When the agent came on the line, Dubois said: 'It worked. The price was high, but he succeeded. Michael Quinn and his PIRA friend, Mick Treacy, were both found dead this morning in a field in south Armagh, shot fatally with 9mm bullets. A total of thirteen shots. Cranfield took them out before being mortally wounded. His own killers are unknown.'

Dubois stopped speaking to listen to the response. When the agent congratulated him, he smiled and hung up, clasped his fingers beneath his chin, pursed his lips for a moment, then smiled again and pressed the button on his intercom.

'It's going to be a nice day,' he told his secretary. 'I'll have tea and biscuits now.'

'Yes, sir,' she replied.

Pleased, Dubois released the intercom button and

leaned back in his chair.

'A *very* nice day!' he whispered.

Sitting between his mates in the cramped rear o
the armoured pig taking them along the M1, secure
in his body armour, checking his Heckler & Koch
MP5 and adjusting his respirator, Ricketts glanced
out the back and saw the sun rising over the soft
green hills on both sides of the motorway. He also
saw the Gazelles coming down on the overt OPs,
bringing resups and replacement troops, before
lifting off the men who had been there all night or,
in certain cases, for many days and nights. Ricketts
still found it hard to believe that those lovely hills
were a killing ground and that of all the places he
had fought in, this was the worst. Luckily, he was
fighting it with some good mates, which made all
the difference.

'Are you OK?' Lampton asked him.

'Yes, Frank, I'm fine. A rude shock to have this
unexpected call, but I'm waking up now.'

'I'd love to know where Cranfield is.'

'He's been missing since yesterday.'

'I asked Captain Dubois and he said that it wasn't
my business. I felt like smacking his face.'

'An Army ponce,' Gumboot said. 'He's never
been in the SAS. He still thinks the lower ranks
and NCOs should be kept in their place. Little does
he know.'

'A good soldier, though,' Martin said. 'I mean he

as a good record. He's been in Northern Ireland a long time and done a lot of good.'

'We did a lot of good in Oman,' Gumboot replied, 'but no one's singing *our* praises.'

'You know what I mean,' Martin said.

'Och, aye,' Jock cut in with an exaggerated Scottish accent. 'We all know that him and Cranfield are your heroes. That must mean you're officer material and all set to move on. The best o' luck, laddy.'

'Leave him alone,' Lampton said. 'Martin's earned his badge just by being here. He's also proven himself to be a good soldier, so let him have heroes. And let him be a good officer if that's what he wants.'

'Sure, boss,' Jock replied, rolling his eyes, shaking his head and flashing Gumboot a 'What more can I say?' look. 'Anything you say, boss.'

But no matter how much they mocked him, Martin was pleased to hear Sergeant Lampton speaking about him that way. He was proud of how he had behaved here – particularly during the first encounter with PIRA youths from the Divis flats – though he knew that not everyone in the Troop thought that highly of him.

He didn't mind being sneered at by the likes of Jock and Gumboot – he knew they were working-class, in the SAS for life, and highly resentful of most officers – whom they termed 'short-term Ruperts' – as well as of Troopers who aspired to be one of that class. No, what bothered Martin most was when

Troopers his own age – and, like him, only recently badged – behaved exactly the same way.

Officers like Cranfield and Dubois were indeed what Martin aspired to be. They represented his future. The other men, Martin realized, didn't understand such ambitions and strongly resented anyone who harboured them.

'I think Cranfield's gone looking for Michael Quinn,' Martin said distractedly, still thinking about the wedge his ambition drove between him and the other Troopers.

'Probably,' Taff Burgess said. 'Our surveillance proved that he had a bug about him – you know, Public Enemy Number One. He was stung that Quinn managed to get away, so he's probably gone after him.'

'The dumb shit,' Dead-eye said. They were the first words he had spoken. 'You ask me, *all* officers are dumb shits.' He shrugged. 'Who gives a fuck?'

'I do,' Lampton replied. 'I don't like big-timers. To tell you the truth, Lieutenant Cranfield has me worried. Where the fuck is he?'

'Somewhere he shouldn't be,' Ricketts replied. 'You can bet your life on it.'

'I don't bet,' Dead-eye said.

Danny looked with admiration at the expression-less Dead-eye and finally got up the courage to ask his burning question.

''Scuse me, Sergeant, do you mind if I ask you something?' Dead-eye just stared flatly at him, not responding at all, so Danny took a deep breath and came right out with it: 'What kind of experience did you have in the Telok Anson swamp in Malaya?'

The ensuing silence was filled only by the low growling of the armoured pig's engine and the wind roaring outside. Jock glanced at Gumboot, who rolled his eyes and whistled softly. Ricketts and Lampton exchanged glances, then lowered their heads to grin. Taff Burgess, who was terrified of Dead-eye, looked down at his boots, while Martin, who was also frightened of him, looked on, fascinated.

Eventually, after what seemed like an eternity, Dead-eye, staring flatly at Danny, said: 'What do you mean, kid?'

Danny cleared his throat, stoking his courage. 'I mean, you're really quiet, you know? And really good – a great soldier. I mean, you never say nothing – you just *do* it – but you do it so well and you learnt it all in that swamp in Malaya. I hear it changed you . . . you were changed in that jungle. What happened there, Sarge?'

Dead-eye stared at Danny for a long time, his eyes as flat as two stones; then speaking in what sounded like the voice of the walking dead, he said: 'It rained and it was hot and it stank and it was dark; and we lived off the jungle and shat and pissed in the water and fought the fucking guerrillas as ordered. What more do you need to know?'

'Nothing.'

'Good,' Dead-eye said.

No one spoke after that.

As the armoured pig trundled off the A1, cut through the Broadway, and turned into the Falls Road, Ricketts was reminded again of just how much he detested being in Northern Ireland. This wasn't a real war with an enemy to respect, but a dirty game of hide and seek, a demeaning police action, a bloody skirmish against faceless killers, mean-faced adolescents, hate-filled children and contemptuous housewives. Christ, he loathed it.

Ricketts was filled with this disgust as the armoured pig took him through the mean streets of Belfast in dawn's pale light, past terraced houses with doors and windows bricked up, pubs barricaded with concrete blocks and off-licences, betting shops and all kinds of shops protected by coils of barbed wire. He did, however, manage to swallow his bile when they neared the estate and Sergeant Lampton, now his best friend, started counting off the distance to the leap: 'Two hundred metres . . . one hundred . . . fifty metres . . . *Go! Go! Go!*'

The armoured pig screeched to a halt, its rear doors burst open, and the men, including Ricketts, leapt out one by one, carrying their weapons in the Belfast Cradle, then raced across the debris-strewn lawns in front of the bleak blocks of flats, still wreathed in the early-morning mist.

Ricketts raced ahead with Lampton, across the

lawn, into the block, along the litter-filled walkway, even as someone shouted a warning – a child's voice, loud and high-pitched – and a door slammed shut just above.

Up a spiral of steps, along a covered balcony, boots clattering on the concrete, making a hell of a racket, then Lampton was at the door in front of Ricketts, taking aim at the lock with his Remington 870 pump-action shotgun.

The noise was ear-splitting, echoing under the balcony's ceiling, as the wood around the Yale lock splintered and the door was kicked open. Lampton dropped to his knees, lowering the Remington, taking aim with his Browning High Power as Ricketts rushed into the room, his Heckler & Koch MP5 at the ready, bawling: 'Security Forces! Don't move!' even as he hurled a stun grenade to confuse those inside.

The grenade exploded, cracking the walls and ceiling, but when its flash had faded away an empty room was revealed.

Cursing, Ricketts and the others rushed through the poky rooms, tearing down the curtains, kicking over tables and chairs, ensuring that no one was hiding anywhere, then covering each other as they backed out again, cursing in frustration.

'Let's try the flats next door!' Gumboot bawled, his voice distorted eerily by the respirator. 'The fuckers on either side!'

But before they could do so, other doors opened

and housewives stepped out, still wearing their nightdresses, curlers in their hair, swearing just like the SAS men, and bending over to drum metal dustbin lids on the brick walls and concrete floor of the balcony.

The noise was deafening, growing louder every second, as more women emerged to do the same, followed by their children.

Their shrieked obscenities added dramatically to the general bedlam until, as Ricketts knew would eventually happen, the first bottle was thrown.

'Damn!' Lampton said, glancing up and down the walkway, then over the concrete wall, the shotgun in one hand, the Browning in the other, but briefly forgetting all he had been taught and failing to watch his own back. 'Let's get the hell out of here.'

It was his first and last mistake.

A ragged, gaunt-faced adolescent had followed them up the stairs and now stepped out of the stairwell with his Webley pistol aimed right at Lampton. He fired three times, in rapid succession, and Lampton was thrown back, bouncing against the concrete wall, even as the kid disappeared again.

Lampton dropped both his weapons and quivered epileptically, blood bursting from his respirator, and was falling as Ricketts raced to the stairs, bawling: 'Christ! Pick him up and let's go!' Then, as bottles burst about him, with drumming binlids and shrieked obscenities resounding in his head, he chased the assassin, plunging into the dangerous gloom of the stairwell without thinking about it.

The stairwell was almost dark, littered with rubbish, stained with piss, its concrete walls covered with graffiti, much of which was political. It was dangerously narrow, each flight of steps short, and Ricketts knew that he was running down blind, with the kid likely to step out from around a corner and blow his head off.

He didn't give a damn. This was a shocking revelation. The strain of the Falls Road OP had already taken its toll, straining his nerves to the limit, and now the shooting of Lampton, his best friend, had made him explode. He knew it, but he couldn't stop himself, so he kept running down the stairs.

'Phil!' Gumboot bellowed from up above.

Ricketts burst out of the stairwell, back into the morning light, just as someone on a balcony above dropped another bottle.

It exploded into a searing, crackling wall of yellow flame about ten metres away. A Molotov cocktail.

The kid with the gun had vanished. Ricketts cursed. When another Molotov cocktail exploded to his right, he glanced up and saw a bunch of dickers hanging over the wall of the balcony, some throwing more bottles. The bottles, which were more home-made petrol bombs, smashed on the ground along the bottom of the block of flats, creating a long wall of yellow fire.

'Shit!' Ricketts said, removing the respirator from his face and letting it dangle under his chin. 'Murderous little bastards!'

He was shocked by the realization that he had almost lost control of himself for the first time since joining the SAS.

'Damn!' he said. 'What the . . .?'

Gumboot came rushing out of the stairwell, crouched low, his Colt Commando at the ready.

'Jesus, Ricketts!' he exclaimed. 'What the hell do you think you're doing, going down the stairwell without back-up? You could have got yourself killed.'

'Sorry. I lost my head for a moment. Is Lampton . . .?'

Before Gumboot could reply, Jock McGregor appeared, carrying the blood-soaked Lampton over his shoulders.

'He's dead,' Gumboot said.

Ricketts felt terrible grief and rage, one emotion at odds with the other, but before he could think about it the wall beside him exploded, spitting dust and pulverized mortar, and he realized that he'd heard a rifle firing.

'Sniper!' Gumboot bellowed, dropping to his knees and scanning the waste ground as Jock hurried towards the armoured pig, still carrying Lampton. 'Some bastard up on the roof! Let's get the fuck out of here!'

Ricketts glanced back at the flats and saw smoke

billowing up from the balconies, forcing the dickers and housewives to scatter, many of them obviously choking and trying to cover their streaming eyes and noses. The roaring of sub-machine-guns suddenly came from the stairwell, then Danny and Taff came backing out, firing as they retreated.

'What's happening?' Ricketts shouted.

'We were covering Jock,' Taff said, 'as he carried Lampton down, with Dead-eye and Martin trying to hold back those stupid bastards on the second floor. They'd started throwing Molotov cocktails and instead of getting us they set fire to their own bloody flats. We backed down the stairs as Dead-eye and Danny threw some CS grenades and fired some rubber bullets, trying to hold the mob back. Then, just as we reached the stairwell leading down from the first floor, another bunch – hard men, not kids – carrying spiked clubs and chains, came along the first-floor balcony. Some followed us down the stairwell; the others went up to the second floor. Now Dead-eye and Martin are trapped up there, caught between the two groups. I think we have to go back up.'

Ricketts glanced back at the armoured pig to see Jock leaning forward, into the open rear doors, letting Lampton's body roll into the vehicle. 'Come on, Gumboot, let's go,' he shouted.

'What about us?' Danny asked.

Ricketts glanced at the wall of flame that ran

along the front of the building, sending up a great column of black smoke.

'There should be another entrance at the far end of the block,' he said to Danny. 'Go along there, take the stairs to the second floor, and come up behind those damned kids.'

'How do I stop them?'

'No bullets. Use a combination of smoke and stun grenades to put them out of action. If necessary, use the butt of your gun to beat the shit out of them.' He glanced back towards the pig and saw Jock at the PRC 319 radio. 'Jock's calling for back-up,' he said. 'It'll come from the nearest RUC station, which is just down the Falls, so it shouldn't take long. Now get up there and calm them down.'

'Right, boss,' Danny said.

While Danny and Taff ran towards the far end of the block of flats, Ricketts and Gumboot rushed back into the stairwell, holding their weapons at the ready, wondering what they would find there.

In fact, the stairwells were empty and they soon reached the second floor.

Martin felt as if he had wings and was taking flight. Standing beside Dead-eye, in the narrow, litter-strewn balcony, caught between the bottle-hurling youths at one end, the screaming housewives in their doorways, the wooden doors set alight by the hastily thrown Molotov cocktails, and the gang of hard men advancing from the other end with spiked clubs and bicycle chains, he was too enraptured with the sheer excitement of it all to feel any fear. This is what he had joined the SAS for and it was more than enough.

He was standing back to back with Dead-eye, facing the oncoming youths as Dead-eye prepared to tackle the hard men. The screaming housewives were dousing the fires with buckets of water, creating more smoke.

Martin asked: 'Do we fire or not, Sarge? I say let's shoot a few of the bastards and set an example.'

'Stop talking shit,' Dead-eye said, sounding calm. 'Shoot one of these bastards and the rest will go mad. Put your respirator on and then throw a couple of hand grenades – a stun grenade, followed by CS. That should dampen their spirits.'

An egg broke against Martin's face. It was followed by some tomatoes. A fat whore of a housewife threw a pile of rubbish at him and someone else deluged him in cold water. His rage came out of nowhere.

'Bugger this,' he said. 'I'm not playing with rubber bullets. If these paddies want to behave like pigs, then I'll treat them that way. I'm not taking this shit!'

'No real bullets!' Dead-eye hissed, as his stun grenade exploded just in front of the hard men, blinding them with light, deafening them, making them reel drunkenly and fall against the walls. It was followed instantly by the CS grenade, which obscured them in a chemical smoke that burned their throats and eyes, hurt their ears and made them choke and vomit.

When one of the youths aimed a pistol at Martin, he let rip with his short-barrelled Sterling sub-machine-gun, firing a short, deadly burst of 9mm bullets.

'No!' Dead-eye bawled.

The young man flung his hands up, looking very surprised, then back-flipped into the group bunched up behind him, parting them like skittles as he crashed backwards on to the concrete floor, his chest pumping blood.

The other youths looked down at him, briefly shocked into immobility, then, realizing that he was already dead, rushed as one at Martin. Being too surprised to fire his weapon a second time, the trooper let them swarm all over him before he could decide what to do.

By then it was too late.

The sub-machine-gun was torn from his hands. His respirator was torn off. He was punched and kicked, then picked up and spun around. He caught a brief glimpse of Dead-eye, whose back was still turned to him, heading boldly into the clouds of CS gas, to beat his way out through the crowd of choking, vomiting hard men.

Martin caught this glimpse of Dead-eye before he was turned away, balanced precariously on the hands of the bawling youths. Then he saw the balcony wall, the ground far below, and knew, with a terrible, lacerating fear, what they were going to do.

He couldn't believe it.

His own scream was the last thing he heard as they heaved him over the balcony and he plunged to the ground.

'Oh, my God!' Taff exclaimed just as he and Danny reached the second floor. 'They've thrown someone off the bloody balcony. Oh, Christ, it's a trooper!'

Danny glanced over the wall and saw the soldier on the ground, face down and not moving a muscle, looking like a rag doll. When he stared along the balcony, he saw some youths running towards him, out of a cloud of CS gas, choking, coughing, wiping their eyes and noses, some falling against the walls, others collapsing, writhing on the ground in their own vomit. Beyond them, Dead-eye was making his escape, beating his way through a gang of older men, all of whom were also suffering badly from the clouds of CS gas.

Clearly, Dead-eye was all right.

When a rifle shot rang out from the roof, Jock twisted sideways, grabbed his left arm, fell to his knees and shook his head as if dazed.

'Go back down and look after them,' Danny said. 'I'm going up on the roof.'

'What?'

'There's a sniper up there and I'm going to get him.'

'I'll come with you.'

'No. You go back down and look after those two.'

'OK,' Taff said. 'Be careful.'

'I will,' Danny replied.

While Taff hurried back down, Danny took the stairs to the roof. It was another three flights up and he passed a few people – two housewives and a pimply-faced youth who wanted to see what was happening. Danny simply brushed past them, pretending they weren't there; but when an older man, bumping into him near the top of the last stairwell, tried to stop him from going further, Danny belted him in the stomach with the stock of his sub-machine-gun, then thumped him on the side of the head and the back of the neck. When the man collapsed, groaning, Danny jumped over him and continued on up the stairs until he burst out on to the roof.

It was a broad, flat expanse filled with water tanks, TV aerials and litter. Plaster had fallen off the brick walls and thick dust covered all.

The sniper was leaning on the front wall, peering into the sights of his .303 Lee Enfield bolt-action sniper rifle. So dedicated was he, so intent on his work, that he didn't even hear Danny's approach until he was practically standing over him.

'Security Forces,' Danny said. 'Don't move!'

The man jerked his head around and looked up in surprise. He was a hard man, all right, with a scarred face and gelid gaze, his surprise soon giving way to fearless contempt. He studied Danny for a moment, taking note of his baby face, then grinned crookedly and said: 'Who the fuck are you kidding, boyo? Could you shoot me this close up?'

'I just might,' Danny said, lowering his sub-machine-gun and removing his Browning from its holster. He raised the handgun and aimed it right between the man's eyes. 'What do *you* think?' he asked.

Still kneeling on the ground, the man turned away from the wall. He deliberately swung the barrel of his rifle towards Danny, resting the stock against his hip for support.

'I think you're about eighteen years old and couldn't shoot someone this close.'

'You may be right,' Danny said.

When the man swung the barrel up higher, preparing to fire, Danny calmly squeezed the trigger of his Browning, putting a burst into the man's chest, directly over the heart. He was punched into the wall, his rifle clattering to the floor, and was dead before the reverberation of the gunshots had faded away.

Danny holstered his handgun, put down his sub-machine-gun, searched the dead man, carefully removing any papers that would help to identify him, then picked his sub-machine-gun up again and walked slowly, cautiously, back down the stairs.

Ricketts and Gumboot had also just reached the second floor when they saw an SAS trooper being flung off the roof and crash with a dreadful thud on to the concrete sixty feet below. They stopped momentarily, frozen with shock, as Jock raced away from the protection of the armoured pig, across the open road, to check that the fallen man was actually dead. Then the sniper fired again, wounding Jock in the arm, making him jerk violently sideways and fall to his knees.

'Oh, those bastards!' Gumboot exclaimed softly. 'I better go back down.'

'No,' Ricketts said. 'Taff's beaten you to it. He'll take care of Jock and ...' He couldn't finish the sentence, not yet knowing exactly who'd been thrown off the roof, so he just shook his head and said: 'Come on. Let's get the hell up there.'

They ran up the remaining stairs and arrived at the third floor just as Dead-eye was advancing towards them. His face was covered with a respirator and he was using the butt of his Colt Commando to beat his way through a crowd of men who were coughing and vomiting in clouds of CS gas. Some of them were falling to the ground and gasping like beached fish.

When Dead-eye reached Ricketts and Gumboot,

ust out of range of the CS gas, he removed the respirator from his face and said: 'They threw Martin off the roof when he shot and killed one of them.'

'He killed one?' Ricketts asked.

'Yes,' Dead-eye said. 'A kid.'

'Oh, Christ!' Ricketts said 'This could cause a lot of trouble.'

'We can counterbalance the kid's death with the story of our man thrown off the roof,' Dead-eye said in a cold-blooded, pragmatic manner. 'That should make them shut up.'

'Fuck,' Ricketts said, feeling shocked and unsure of himself. 'This is one filthy war.'

'It's a pisser,' Gumboot said, 'but we're stuck with it. Now let's get the hell out of here before those bastards recover.' He nodded towards the hard men now choking, vomiting and collapsing in the gas-filled walkway.

'Right,' Dead-eye said. 'Let's go.'

They hurried back down the stairs and out into the road where the fires from the Molotov cocktails were flickering out and two RUC trucks were disgorging men wearing flak jackets and carrying anti-riot shields and truncheons.

As the Quick Reaction Force men raced into the block of flats, sealing off both exits, Jock climbed shakily to his feet, holding his wounded arm, and Taff carried Martin's dead, smashed-up body back to the armoured pig.

Ricketts, Dead-eye and Gumboot formed a protective circle around Jock as he crossed the dangerous stretch of open ground.

They broke apart and spun around, preparing to fire, when they heard the sound of gunfire on the roof.

'That fucking sniper!' Gumboot exclaimed.

'No,' Ricketts said. 'It was a weapon firing on the roof, but it wasn't aimed at us.'

'It was either Danny firing at the sniper,' Taff explained, 'or the sniper firing at him.'

'He's a good kid,' Dead-eye said with a rare, if veiled, display of admiration. 'He'll be OK.'

Dead-eye was rarely wrong.

When Danny materialized, smiling shyly as he told them that the sniper was dead, they all piled gratefully into the armoured pig and were driven back to Bessbrook.

There, while still trying to adjust to the deaths of Frank Lampton and Martin Renshaw, they learned from Captain Dubois that Lieutenant Cranfield had been found at first light, his body riddled with bullets, lying near the dead bodies of PIRA activists Michael Quinn and Mick Treacy.

As the latter pair had been killed with 9mm bullets, six in Quinn, the other seven in Treacy, it was believed that they had both been shot by Cranfield just before he was killed.

It was also believed that Cranfield's Browning,

which had not been found at the scene of the killings, had been stolen by his executioners.

The identity of Cranfield's executioners had yet to be ascertained.

'Last but not least,' Dubois told the assembled men, 'I should inform you that for reasons to do with recent events, you will all soon be transferred back to Hereford. D Squadron will arrive a few weeks later and take over your duties. That's all. Dismissed.'

'Thanks a million,' Jock whispered.

The men left the briefing room, went straight to the NAAFI canteen, steadily drank themselves into a state of sleep-inducing oblivion, then staggered back to their makeshift beds in the Portakabin being used as sleeping quarters. By lights out, they were snoring.

All except Ricketts.

Deeply shocked by the death of Lampton, his best friend since Oman, and also disturbed by the manner of Renshaw's death, Ricketts had trouble sleeping. When at last he did so, after much tossing and turning, he had the first of the nightmares that would haunt him for years to come.

18

The remaining members of the SAS troop were shipped out of Belfast as quietly as they had been shipped in and returned to their Hereford HQ. A few weeks later, when the shock waves from the death of Lieutenant Cranfield had died away, the full complement of D Squadron 22 SAS arrived in Belfast amid a great deal of publicity designed to intimidate the IRA.

The two PIRA youths responsible for Cranfield's death were later caught, convicted and jailed in the Republic. In prison, one of the assassins admitted to Cranfield's controller that he had been present at the ghastly torture of Cranfield, but that the SAS officer had bravely refused to talk.

This knowledge went a long way to restoring Cranfield's tarnished reputation with the other members of the Regiment.

Having learnt from the mistakes of the first small group of SAS men in Northern Ireland, D Squadron chalked up a more satisfying record of counter-terrorist successes, reaping a rich harvest from the seeds sown by their relatively inexperienced, path-finding predecessors. Nevertheless, things did not go smoothly at first, even for D Squadron.

In April 1976 a four-man SAS team was set up in two OPs for surveillance of the house of Peter Cleary, an IRA 'staff captain' who lived near the border. During their many long days and nights in the OPs, the four soldiers had very little sleep and were exposed to the bitter elements.

Early one evening, shortly after a helicopter landing at Crossmaglen was attacked by the IRA with rockets and machine guns, the troopers arrested Cleary in his house near Forkhill, a mere fifty metres north of the border.

Cleary was taken to a nearby field with a five-man SAS escort, to await the arrival of another helicopter. According to one of the soldiers, all of the SAS men but one were used to help guide the chopper down with the aid of torches, which meant that Cleary was being guarded by just one trooper. Seeing his opportunity, he grabbed the soldier's rifle by the barrel and tried to pull it away. The soldier squeezed the trigger three times, hitting Cleary in the chest and killing him instantly.

As being 'shot while trying to escape' is an old military cliché often covering summary execution, few Republicans believed the SAS version of Cleary's death. Though the authorities put the death down to 'insufficient manpower' and 'a lack of handcuffs', the IRA alleged that Cleary had been murdered.

This was another set-back for the SAS.

D Squadron, however, then scored a major victory over the IRA. In early 1977, a young lance-corporal of the Royal Highland Fusiliers was killed by an IRA mortar bomb at Crossmaglen. The only clue to the identity of the killers was a dark-blue Datsun with a black vinyl roof, seen in the vicinity at the time of the incident and believed to be a scout vehicle for the ASU mortar team.

Midway through that month, late one Sunday afternoon, the vehicle was spotted again near the border. A hooded man carrying a bandolier of ammunition and a sawn-off shotgun got out of the car and walked in the direction of the hidden SAS patrol set up to entrap him. When one of the patrol rose to challenge the man, he raised his shotgun to fire. The SAS trooper opened fire first, killing the terrorist.

Immediately, the SAS trooper came under fire from a number of hidden gunmen using high-velocity Armalite rifles. The shots missed their target and the trooper ducked for cover. At the same time, other members of the SAS patrol fired back, aiming at the muzzle-flash of the enemy weapons and eventually forcing the IRA men to flee. When the SAS team went in pursuit of them, they found a trail of blood beside the road.

The man they had shot turned out to be a

wenty-year-old labourer, Seamus Harvey, from nearby Drummakaval. He died less than 200 yards from the site of an ambush in which three British soldiers had been killed just before the SAS arrived to set up their OP.

According to one unnamed source, some of Harvey's wounds were caused by an IRA Armalite rifle later used to murder a UDR corporal.

Because of these operations, IRA attacks in south Armagh ended for almost a year.

The SAS soldiers who had been caught by the Gardai when trying to cross the border into the Republic were returned from Hereford by RAF transport to be put on trial in Dublin. Throughout the trial, they were guarded by a senior SAS officer who let it be known that he feared for their lives. After a tense two days in the courtroom, three judges found the men guilty of entering the Republic without permission, but cleared them on the more serious charge of possessing firearms to endanger life. The weapons used as evidence during the trial were therefore returned to the SAS and the troopers were freed and flown back to Hereford, via RAF Northolt.

This was another victory for the SAS.

Celebrating in the bar at Hereford, Sergeant 'Dead-eye Dick' Parker, Corporal Phil Ricketts, and Troopers 'Jock' McGregor, 'Gumboot' Gillis, 'Taff' Burgess and Danny 'Baby Face' Porter raised their glasses in a toast. Then, though they normally didn't discuss the dead, or those who 'beat the clock', they somehow raised the name of Lieutenant Cranfield, agreeing that although he had certainly been a 'big-timer', he had made amends for it by showing exemplary courage during his final, terrible hours.

'He was a decent man at heart,' Ricketts said, 'but too wayward, or impulsive, for his own good – or for the good of the Regiment.'

'I agree,' Jock said. 'Even if he'd survived, he'd never have been invited back to the Regiment after serving out his first three-year stint.'

'No way,' Gumboot said.

Perhaps in order to avoid the names of the late Frank Lampton and Martin Renshaw, the former widely respected, the latter more reservedly so, they discussed the relationship between the SAS and the intelligence services in Northern Ireland. Their conclusion was that it was complex, bewildering, sometimes unsavoury, and too often deadly.

This led them back to Captain Dubois of 14 Intelligence Company and the mystery of his love-hate relationship with Lieutenant Cranfield.

'That Captain Dubois outsmarted Cranfield,' Ricketts explained, giving utterance at last to one of the many thoughts that had haunted him in past months and led to an increasing number of nightmares. 'I think he knew what he was doing all along. He understood that Cranfield was an unusual kind of SAS officer – impetuous, sometimes thoughtless, prepared to break all the rules – so he et him up to take out Michael Quinn . . . and to do so in a way that would make us look culpable, while absolving the Army from all blame.'

'Well, he certainly succeeded,' Taff offered. 'You've got to admire him.'

'Who dares wins,' Dead-eye said.

OTHER BOOKS IN THIS SERIES

Available now at newsagents and bookseller

SOLDIER A SAS: Behind Iraqi
Lines
£4.99 net

SOLDIER B SAS: Heroes of the
South Atlantic
£4.99 ne

SOLDIER C SAS: Secret War
in Arabia
£4.99 ne

SOLDIER D SAS: The Colombian
Cocaine War
£4.99 ne

SOLDIER F SAS: Guerrillas in
the Jungle
£4.99 net